Scholastic Success With

TESTS

READING

WORKBOOK

GRADE 4

From the Editors of *Scholastic News*

SCHOLASTIC
PROFESSIONAL BOOKS

New York ⊙ Toronto ⊙ London ⊙ Auckland ⊙ Sydney
Mexico City ⊙ New Delhi ⊙ Hong Kong ⊙ Buenos Aires

The *Scholastic Success With Tests: Reading* series is designed to help you help students succeed on standardized tests. In this workbook for fourth grade, the 15, four-page tests are culled from the reading skills practice tests provided three times a year to *Scholastic News Edition 4* subscribers, with some new and revised material. By familiarizing children with the skills, language, and formats they will encounter on state and national tests like the Terra Nova, ITBS, CTBS, and MAT, these practice tests will boost confidence and help raise scores.

The questions supporting each test are specifically designed to review the following skills:

- Finding the Main Idea
- Reading for Detail
- Understanding Vocabulary
- Making Inferences
- Sequencing
- Understanding Cause and Effect
- Understanding Author's Purpose
- Understanding Fact and Opinion

Note that the tests in the second half of the book are slightly more difficult. These are designed to be given later in the school year.

In addition to helping children prepare for "real" tests, the practice tests in this workbook may be used as a diagnostic tool, to help you detect individual students' strengths and weaknesses, or as an instructional tool, for oral reading and discussion.

Keep in mind that our practice tests are just that—practice. These tests are not standardized. They should not be used to determine grade level, to compare one student's performance with that of others, or to evaluate teachers' abilities.

HOW TO ADMINISTER THE TESTS:

Before administering each test, you may wish to review with students some basic test-taking strategies, such as reading the questions before reading the passages.

- Establish a relaxed atmosphere. Explain to students that they will not be graded and that they are taking the test to practice for "real" tests down the road.
- Review the directions, then read the samples in each section and discuss the answers. Be sure to pay close attention to the directions in the vocabulary section on the last page of each test.
- To mimic the atmosphere of a real test, you may wish to set time limits. Students should be able to complete the reading comprehension section (the first three pages of each test) in 20 to 25 minutes. Allow an additional 10 minutes for the vocabulary portion on the last page of each test.
- Use the **Answer Key** provided on pages 63-64 to check students' work; or if desired, have students check their own answers.

Cover design by Maria Lilja • Cover art by Victoria Raymond
ISBN 0-439-42575-1
Copyright © 2002 by Scholastic Inc. All rights reserved. Printed in the USA.
8 9 10   40   08 07 06

Reading Skills Practice Test I

READING COMPREHENSION

Read each story. Then fill in the circle that best completes each sentence or answers each question.

SAMPLE

Many people like to glide along the sidewalk on roller skates. They owe a vote of thanks to Joseph Merlin of Belgium. He invented a kind of roller skate back in 1760. His skates **provided** a pretty bumpy ride, however.

I. What is the best title for this story?
- ○ **A.** "Inventors"
- ○ **B.** "Famous Inventions"
- ○ **C.** "Belgium"
- ○ **D.** "Early Roller Skates"

2. In this story, the word **provided** means
- ○ **A.** scraped.
- ○ **B.** invented.
- ○ **C.** gave
- ○ **D.** took

A. Boston Post Road is the oldest road in the United States. It is more than 300 years old! Colonists made the road in the 1670s, more than 100 years before American Revolution. They needed a way to carry mail and messages between two growing cities—Boston and New York. The road followed old Native American trails.

I. What is the best title for this story?
- ○ **A.** "Building Roads"
- ○ **B.** "U.S. Mail"
- ○ **C.** "Two Colonial Cities"
- ○ **D.** "America's First Road"

2. You can guess that
- ○ **A.** Boston Post Road is still around.
- ○ **B.** Boston is a small city.
- ○ **C.** Boston Post Road is short.
- ○ **D.** New York is older than Boston.

3. You would probably find this story in a book about
- ○ **A.** fairy tales.
- ○ **B.** current events.
- ○ **C.** how to build roads.
- ○ **D.** American history.

B. In 1271, Marco Polo left Italy and set out for China. He was just 17 years old! Polo's trip took three and a half years. In China, he discovered a black stone that burned and gave heat. It was coal. Polo also learned about paper-making and the compass. When he got home, he wrote a book about his **journey**.

I. Marco Polo traveled to
○ **A.** Greece.
○ **B.** the United States.
○ **C.** China.
○ **D.** Africa.

2. In this story, the word **journey** means
○ **A.** trip.
○ **B.** findings.
○ **C.** sailboat.
○ **D.** country.

3. Which of these is an *opinion* about Marco Polo?
○ **A.** He lived in the 1200s.
○ **B.** He traveled to China
○ **C.** He was the greatest explorer of all time.
○ **D.** He wrote a book.

C. When you're hungry, or even just thinking about food, you often hear your stomach growl. Sometimes, your stomach also growls when you're nervous or excited. What you are actually hearing is your stomach muscles pushing air around inside your stomach.

Your stomach also makes noises right after you eat. That's because your stomach muscles move around to mix the food you're eaten with special juices. When they do this, they also move around the air that you swallowed with your food. This causes your stomach to growl, though not as loudly as when your stomach is empty.

I. This story is mainly about
○ **A.** how you digest food.
○ **B.** muscles of the human body.
○ **C.** why your stomach growls.
○ **D.** why people get hungry.

2. You can guess that your stomach growls the loudest when you
○ **A.** are eating.
○ **B.** are at school.
○ **C.** yell loudly.
○ **D.** need food.

3. Which of the following statements is an *opinion*?
○ **A.** Stomach noises are gross.
○ **B.** Your stomach growls when its muscles push air around in your stomach.
○ **C.** Your stomach can growl when it's full.
○ **D.** Sometimes your stomach growls when you're nervous.

4. Your stomach growls because
○ **A.** you have eaten too much.
○ **B.** there is air in your stomach.
○ **C.** you feel sick to your stomach.
○ **D.** you are tired.

D. More than 40 fish produce electricity. The most dangerous is the electric eel, a long slimy fish that lives in South America. This snakelike fish gives off electric signals to "see" in the dark water where it lives. These signals bounce off underwater objects and help the eel find fish and frogs to eat.

Once the electric eel **locates** its prey, it fills the water with an electric shock. The organs that produce electricity are in the eel's tail. The shock stuns or kills any small animals in the area around the eel. The electric charge is so strong it could also stun a person or knock over a full-grown horse!

1. The electric eel looks like a
- ○ **A.** snake.
- ○ **B.** fish.
- ○ **C.** turtle.
- ○ **D.** bird.

2. The author wrote this story to
- ○ **A.** tell about different kinds of eels.
- ○ **B.** tell about electric eels.
- ○ **C.** ask people to protect fish.
- ○ **D.** explain electricity.

3. In this story, the word **locates** means
- ○ **A.** swims.
- ○ **B.** eats.
- ○ **C.** slides.
- ○ **D.** finds.

E. Popcorn is one of the oldest American snack foods. By the time European explorers arrived here in the 1400s, Native Americans were already growing about 700 types of corn. They used popcorn for both food and decoration. Some tribes used it in their headdresses and necklaces.

These early popcorn lovers couldn't plug in the electric popper or zap the popcorn in the microwave. Instead, they popped the kernels in clay pots over an open fire. Some kinds of popcorn were even popped right on the cob.

English colonists got a taste of popcorn at the first Thanksgiving feast in 1621. A Native American named Quadequina brought a deerskin bag filled with popcorn to the dinner. It was a hit!

1. What is the best title for this story?
- ○ **A.** "The History of Popcorn"
- ○ **B.** "Native Americans"
- ○ **C.** "The First Thanksgiving"
- ○ **D.** "Snack Foods"

2. Which happened first?
- ○ **A.** Colonists ate popcorn.
- ○ **B.** Electric-poppers were invented.
- ○ **C.** Movie theaters served popcorn.
- ○ **D.** Native Americans grew corn.

3. Popcorn has been used for
- ○ **A.** sewing.
- ○ **B.** making paint.
- ○ **C.** heating homes.
- ○ **D.** making jewelry.

4. This story would probably go on to talk about
- ○ **A.** how microwaves work.
- ○ **B.** the popularity of popcorn today.
- ○ **C.** Native American customs.
- ○ **D.** snacks of the world.

VOCABULARY

Synonyms

Read the underlined word in each phrase.
Mark the word below it that has the same
(or close to the same) meaning.

Sample:

damage the building
- ○ **A.** hurt
- ○ **B.** deck
- ○ **C.** anger
- ○ **D.** command

I. argue about it
- ○ **A.** laugh
- ○ **B.** pickle
- ○ **C.** fight
- ○ **D.** whisper

2. gradually cook
- ○ **A.** boil
- ○ **B.** slowly
- ○ **C.** hot
- ○ **D.** quickly

3. a rose's scent
- ○ **A.** red
- ○ **B.** smell
- ○ **C.** stem
- ○ **D.** color

4. annoy her
- ○ **A.** help
- ○ **B.** necklace
- ○ **C.** bother
- ○ **D.** talk

5. wicked character
- ○ **A.** sweet
- ○ **B.** boy
- ○ **C.** helpful
- ○ **D.** mean

6. unkind words
- ○ **A.** friendly
- ○ **B.** mean
- ○ **C.** happy
- ○ **D.** shy

7. wee child
- ○ **A.** small
- ○ **B.** large
- ○ **C.** happy
- ○ **D.** shy

Antonyms

Read the underlined word in each phrase.
Mark the word below it that means
the opposite or nearly the opposite.

Sample:

silent evening
- ○ **A.** quiet
- ○ **B.** patient
- ○ **C.** noisy
- ○ **B.** perfect

I. worthless watch
- ○ **A.** leather
- ○ **B.** ticking
- ○ **C.** valuable
- ○ **D.** cart

2. afternoon stroll
- ○ **A.** walk
- ○ **B.** sun
- ○ **C.** pond
- ○ **D.** run

3. antique chest
- ○ **A.** brown
- ○ **B.** old
- ○ **C.** case
- ○ **D.** new

4. cheap shoes
- ○ **A.** blue
- ○ **B.** strings
- ○ **C.** expensive
- ○ **D.** free

5. exit the building
- ○ **A.** enter
- ○ **B.** door
- ○ **C.** roof
- ○ **D.** leave

6. vast ocean
- ○ **A.** large
- ○ **B.** tiny
- ○ **C.** deep
- ○ **D.** shallow

7. valuable earrings
- ○ **A.** worthless
- ○ **B.** expensive
- ○ **C.** diamond
- ○ **D.** pendant

Reading Skills Practice Test 2

READING COMPREHENSION

Read each story. Then fill in the circle that best completes each sentence or answers each question.

Many people get nosebleeds. That's because the lining inside the nose is very **sensitive**. Dry air or sneezing can irritate it. If one of the small blood vessels in the lining should break, the blood starts to flow!

1. What is the best title for this story?
- ○ **A.** "Eyes, Ears, Nose, and Throat"
- ○ **B.** "How the Nose Works"
- ○ **C.** "The Sense of Smell"
- ○ **D.** "Why You Get Bloody Noses"

2. In this story, the word **sensitive** means
- ○ **A.** pinkish-red.
- ○ **B.** often bloody.
- ○ **C.** easily hurt.
- ○ **D.** very tough.

A. Labor Day is a special day for many Americans. They get to take the day off! The holiday honors everyone who works in America—even kids!

The first Labor Day was celebrated in 1882. A carpenter named Peter McGuire decided that workers should have a special day to honor them. So he planned a parade for all of the workers in his hometown of New York City. Ten thousand people marched proudly through the streets. That day, they enjoyed music, picnics, and fireworks.

In 1894, President Grover Cleveland made Labor Day a national holiday. It is always the first Monday in September.

1. What is the best title for this story?
- ○ **A.** "My Favorite Labor Day"
- ○ **B.** "Hooray for Parades!"
- ○ **C.** "The History of Labor Day"
- ○ **D.** "Holidays Around the World"

2. Labor Day became a national holiday
- ○ **A.** in 1882.
- ○ **B.** in 1994.
- ○ **C.** last September.
- ○ **D.** in 1894.

3. Which is an *opinion* about Labor Day?
- ○ **A.** It always takes place on a Monday.
- ○ **B.** It is a great holiday.
- ○ **C.** It was started by Peter McGuire.
- ○ **D.** Its purpose is to honor workers.

B. If one of your classmates made fun of you in the schoolyard, or cheated at a game you were playing together, what would you do? Many people would get angry. Some might even start yelling, pushing, or punching.

At 75th Street School in Los Angeles, California, kids in every grade learn how to solve problems without fighting. The school has a team of students called conflict managers who are specially trained.

How do students become conflict managers? First, they must be in grades 4 or 5. Then, teachers and other students must choose them. In the playground, these conflict managers keep an eye out for arguments. They help solve problems when students disagree.

1. This article is mainly about
○ **A.** why kids argue.
○ **B.** schools in California.
○ **C.** one solution to playground fighting.
○ **D.** violence in the community.

2. The conflict managers are
○ **A.** college students.
○ **B.** teachers at 75th Street School.
○ **C.** in 1st or 2nd grade.
○ **D.** in 4th or 5th grade.

3. The story would probably go on to talk about
○ **A.** popular playground games.
○ **B.** how conflict managers handle arguments.
○ **C.** how to do first aid outdoors.
○ **D.** downtown Los Angeles.

C. In honor of Fire Safety Week, here are some fire-safety tips for you to follow:
• Never play with matches or lighters.
• Ask your parents to make sure your home has smoke detectors and a fire extinguisher.
• Make a plan for escaping from your home in case of fire. Learn two ways out of every room. Pick a spot outside where your family will meet. Practice!
• If there is a fire in your home, get out and stay out! Use a neighbor's phone to call for help.
• Find a **route** out of the building that is free from smoke and flames. If you have to go through a smoky area to escape, crawl on your hands and knees. The air near the floor will be cooler and less smoky.
• If your clothes catch fire, do not run. Drop to the ground, and roll back and forth to put out the flames.

1. The purpose of this article is to
○ **A.** explain why fires start.
○ **B.** teach fire safety.
○ **C.** describe what a fire is like.
○ **D.** show how fire can be used safely.

2. In this story, the word **route** means
○ **A.** path.
○ **B.** place.
○ **C.** door.
○ **D.** air.

3. To escape a smoky area, you should
○ **A.** run.
○ **B.** scream.
○ **C.** crawl.
○ **D.** roll back and forth on the ground.

4. Which is a *fact* about fire safety?
○ **A.** You should have fire drills often.
○ **B.** In case of fire, save your toys first.
○ **C.** In a fire, the air is cooler near the floor.
○ **D.** Children should never use matches.

D. Once upon a time, a man lived in a gloomy basement, where he worked all day long. Even so, he was happy because he sang as he worked.

Above the poor man lived a rich man, who worried all day long about his money. This made him miserable. Being in a bad mood, he really hated to hear the poor man singing.

He wanted the poor man to feel bad, like he did. He thought if the poor man felt bad, he might stop singing. He thought if the poor man had money, he too might worry. So the rich man gave the poor man a big sack of money.

The poor man was happier than ever— until he realized that someone might steal the money from him. So he decided to hide it. But no place seemed safe enough. There was nothing he could do—except worry.

The poor man worried until he grew thin and pale. He no longer felt like singing.

One day, he gave the money back to the rich man. "I can live without this money," he said. "But I cannot live without my song."

1. This story tells why
- ○ **A.** a poor man had no money.
- ○ **B.** money made a poor man unhappy.
- ○ **C.** a rich man loved his money
- ○ **D.** money made a poor man sing.

2. The rich man gave the poor man money
- ○ **A.** to make him happy.
- ○ **B.** to make him sing more.
- ○ **C.** to make him worry.
- ○ **D.** to make him move away.

3. Which happened last?
- ○ **A.** The rich man worried all day long.
- ○ **B.** The poor man gave back the money.
- ○ **C.** The poor man stopped singing.
- ○ **D.** The rich man gave the poor man a big sack of money.

E. Once the howl of the wolf was heard all over the United States' wilderness. But by 1900, only a few thousand wolves roamed free in the U.S. In 1973, the government put wolves on the endangered-species list.

Today, animal activists are working to bring back the wolf. As an experiment, 31 wild wolves from Canada were released in Yellowstone National Park. Nine wolf pups were born there. Now, animal activists want to repeat this success story in New York, Maine, New Mexico, and Arizona.

But, some farmers and ranchers worry that this meat eater will hunt their **livestock**. In New York, dairy farmers worry that wolves will attack their dairy cows. In New Mexico, ranchers worry about wolf attacks on their cattle and sheep.

1. What is the main idea of this story?
- ○ **A.** The wolf program in Yellowstone was a big success.
- ○ **B.** Although wolves are endangered, not everyone wants to help them.
- ○ **C.** Wolves are meat-eaters.
- ○ **D.** Ranchers and farmer dislike wolves.

2. In this story, the word **livestock** means
- ○ **A.** farmers.   ○ **B.** barns.
- ○ **C.** farm animals.   ○ **D.** grass.

3. From this article, you could guess that wolves
- ○ **A.** are dangerous to people.
- ○ **B.** like sheep better than cows.
- ○ **C.** are happier in Canada.
- ○ **D.** might roam into ranches or farms.

VOCABULARY

Synonyms

Read the underlined word in each phrase. Mark the word below it that has the same (or close to the same) meaning.

Sample:

mend the fence
- A. break
- C. fix
- B. banana
- D. climb

1. rapidly stir
   - A. shake
   - C. mix
   - B. quickly
   - D. slowly

2. the student's task
   - A. smart
   - C. school
   - B. job
   - D. book

3. tore paper
   - A. glued
   - C. ripped
   - B. sheet
   - D. wrote

4. an imaginary friend
   - A. best
   - C. real
   - B. kind
   - D. make-believe

5. a log cabin
   - A. wood
   - C. brown
   - B. house
   - D. room

6. loud wail
   - A. song
   - C. bang
   - B. siren
   - D. cry

7. tilt sideways
   - A. hoe
   - C. straighten
   - B. lean
   - D. tile

Antonyms

Read the underlined word in each phrase. Mark the word below it that means the opposite or nearly the opposite.

Sample:

useless tool
- A. metal
- C. helpful
- B. sharp
- B. hammer

1. loud chuckle
   - A. laugh
   - C. radio
   - B. car
   - D. sob

2. feel ashamed
   - A. embarrassed
   - C. sick
   - B. happy
   - D. proud

3. silent classroom
   - A. noisy
   - C. warm
   - B. teacher
   - D. quiet

4. beneath the roof
   - A. under
   - C. above
   - B. raise
   - D. below

5. a sudden shriek
   - A. scream
   - C. whisper
   - B. reply
   - D. noise

6. a great triumph
   - A. success
   - C. failure
   - B. trial
   - D. finish

7. widen the road
   - A. narrow
   - C. curve
   - B. pave
   - D. straighten

Reading Skills Practice Test 3

READING COMPREHENSION

Read each story. Then fill in the circle that best completes each sentence or answers each question.

SAMPLE

Being bitten by a bedbug stinks in more ways than one. It hurts and the bug gives off a bad odor. These critters, each about the size of a grain of rice, **nourish** themselves on human blood. Their odor prevents other bugs from feasting on bedbugs!

1. What is the best title for this story?
○ **A.** "Why Bedbugs Live in Beds"
○ **B.** "How Bedbugs Live"
○ **C.** "Bugs that Eat Rice"
○ **D.** "Bedbugs Stink"

2. In this story, the word **nourish** means
○ **A.** feed.
○ **B.** clean.
○ **C.** hungry.
○ **D.** stink.

A.   A club called the Graffiti Grapplers won't stand for a mess—especially not in their hometown of San Antonio, Texas. The group of teachers and kids paint over graffiti and sweep up litter in their community.

Since the club was founded in 1993, the Grapplers have won many awards. One year, they won $32,500! The club members use the money they receive for projects such as planting trees and flowers around San Antonio.

"These kids have good hearts," Grappler and teacher Linda Pruski said. "They are seeing the positive effect they can have on the community."

1. What is the best title for this story?
○ **A.** "The History of San Antonio"
○ **B.** "A Club for Kids Who Care"
○ **C.** "The Growing Problem of Graffiti"
○ **D.** "How to Win Big Money"

2. The Graffiti Grapplers club was founded
○ **A.** in 1990.
○ **B.** by teachers and business people.
○ **C.** by graffiti artists.
○ **D.** in Texas.

3. Which of the following is an *opinion* about the Graffiti Grapplers?
○ **A.** Its members are teachers and kids.
○ **B.** It is based in San Antonio, Texas.
○ **C.** It is one of the best clubs in San Antonio.
○ **D.** Its members clean up litter and graffiti.

B. Once upon a time, most people thought the world was flat. Eventually, new discoveries proved them wrong. Scientists have always thought that all planets moved in nearly circular orbits. Now, they believe that idea may be wrong, too.

Why? Just a few years ago, astronomers discovered a planet outside of our solar system that moves around its sun in a very flattened, egg-shaped or oblong path.

The newly discovered planet is 17 times larger than Earth. It was spotted in a constellation called Cygnus, located 600 trillion miles, or about 70 light-years, from Earth. Now scientists are researching to find out what makes this planet move in such a wacky way.

1. The purpose of this article is to
○ **A.** explain why Earth may be flat after all.
○ **B.** show that new discoveries can lead to new ideas.
○ **C.** show that scientists are always right.
○ **D.** discuss how humans could visit Cygnus.

2. In this story, the word oblong means
○ **A.** orbit   ○ **C.** shaped like a circle
○ **B.** egg-shaped   ○ **D.** discovery

3. The newly discovered planet was spotted
○ **A.** in our solar system.
○ **B.** herbivores are small animals.
○ **C.** moving around Earth.
○ **D.** in the constellation Cygnus.

C. Animals can't speak in words, but they have many other ways to "talk" to each other. Here's a look at how several different creatures communicate in the wild.

• Giant otters speak in a unique language of whistles, whines, squeals, and snorts. Each sound means a different thing. For instance, one type of snort warns other otters of danger, such as a nearby human hunter.

• Red howler monkeys communicate by howling. Their howls can be heard up to three miles away. In fact, these monkeys are the world's noisiest land animals.

• Wolves curl their lips above their teeth and snarl at other wolves to show who's in charge, and to warn other wolves to back off. Wolves will also howl to signal danger.

• The elephant seal uses its amazing inflatable nose and its nostrils as a giant microphone.

1. This article is mainly about
○ **A.** why red howler monkeys are so loud.
○ **B.** animals that use their noses to communicate.
○ **C.** ways different animals communicate.
○ **D.** how giant otters stay safe from hunters.

2. According to the article, elephant seals communicate by
○ **A.** inflating their noses.
○ **B.** whistling.
○ **C.** snarling.
○ **D.** wagging their tails.

3. The story would probably go on to talk about
○ **A.** what red howler monkeys eat.
○ **B.** how other animals communicate.
○ **C.** where giant otters live.
○ **D.** how wolves talk to giant otters.

4. Which is a *fact* about animal communication?
○ **A.** The elephant seal's inflatable nose is really strange.
○ **B.** Listening to red howler monkeys all day would really get on your nerves.
○ **C.** Wolves look scary when they snarl.
○ **D.** Whistles and snorts are part of the giant otter's language.

D. What's wet and covers three fourths of the Earth's surface? It's the water that makes up the Earth's four oceans. These oceans are the Pacific, the Atlantic, the Indian, and the Arctic. The Pacific Ocean is the largest and deepest. The Arctic Ocean is the smallest and shallowest.

Oceans are the **source** of many different things people need. Ocean water contains salt, a basic cooking need. Some ocean plants, like seaweed, are used for medicine and food. Ocean fishing provides many people with work and food.

Oceans can also be fun places to visit. People who visit the ocean might swim in the waves, hunt for shells, and play in the sand.

On a map, the Earth's four oceans may look just like giant pools of water. But they are so much more than that.

1. Which ocean is the deepest?
- ○ **A.** the Pacific
- ○ **B.** the Atlantic
- ○ **C.** the Indian
- ○ **D.** the Arctic

2. What is one thing people need that they can get from the ocean?
- ○ **A.** ice
- ○ **B.** salt
- ○ **C.** sand
- ○ **D.** waves

3. How much of the Earth's surface do oceans cover?
- ○ **A.** one third
- ○ **B.** one half
- ○ **C.** two thirds
- ○ **D.** three fourths

4. In this story, the word **source** means
- ○ **A.** store.
- ○ **B.** salty.
- ○ **C.** place to get.
- ○ **D.** place to put.

E. Ghosts and ghouls have raised more than $100 million to help poor children around the world. How? By trick-or-treating!

They were trick-or-treating for UNICEF. UNICEF is the United Nation's Children's Fund.

Founded in 1946, UNICEF has helped children in more than 140 poor or war-torn countries get food, shelter, and medicine. Every year it adopts a new slogan, such as "Increase the Peace!"

A group of kids from Philadelphia founded the trick-or-treat for UNICEF program in 1950. They raised $17. Ever since, kids dressed in their Halloween best have followed suit—and, as the program has grown, the amount of money kids raise has grown far beyond $17 annually. In fact, in a recent year, kids helped raise $2.1 million. This year, they could raise even more!

1. What is the main idea of this story?
- ○ **A.** Halloween is one of kids' favorite holidays.
- ○ **B.** Trick-or-treat for UNICEF is a successful program to raise money for poor children.
- ○ **C.** Trick-or-treat for UNICEF was founded in 1950.
- ○ **D.** Trick-or-treat for UNICEF is no longer a popular program

2. Which happened last?
- ○ **A.** UNICEF was founded.
- ○ **B.** Kids began trick-or-treating for UNICEF.
- ○ **C.** Kids helped raise $2.1 million for UNICEF.
- ○ **D.** A group of kids from Philadelphia raised $17.

3. From this article, you could guess that
- ○ **A.** large numbers of children participate in trick-or-treat for UNICEF.
- ○ **B.** kids from Philadelphia are nicer than most other kids.
- ○ **C.** the trick-or-treat for UNICEF program made more money in the 1950s than it does now.
- ○ **D.** kids get more candy when they trick-or-treat for UNICEF.

VOCABULARY

Synonyms

Read the underlined word in each phrase. Mark the word below it that has the same (or close to the same) meaning.

Sample:

argue loudly
- ○ **A.** agree
- ○ **B.** fight
- ○ **C.** toaster
- ○ **D.** shout

1. current event
   - ○ **A.** funny
   - ○ **B.** article
   - ○ **C.** recent
   - ○ **D.** old

2. sharp fang
   - ○ **A.** tooth
   - ○ **B.** knife
   - ○ **C.** mouth
   - ○ **D.** eat

3. solid foundation
   - ○ **A.** rock
   - ○ **B.** base
   - ○ **C.** breeze
   - ○ **D.** ice

4. eerie sound
   - ○ **A.** loud
   - ○ **B.** spooky
   - ○ **C.** monster
   - ○ **D.** whisper

5. stroll downtown
   - ○ **A.** appear
   - ○ **B.** drive
   - ○ **C.** store
   - ○ **D.** walk

6. false statement
   - ○ **A.** loud
   - ○ **B.** whispered
   - ○ **C.** sworn
   - ○ **D.** untrue

7. blend in
   - ○ **A.** fill
   - ○ **B.** mix
   - ○ **C.** throw
   - ○ **D.** push

Antonyms

Read the underlined word in each phrase. Mark the word below it that means the opposite or nearly the opposite.

Sample:

latch the door
- ○ **A.** unlock
- ○ **B.** slam
- ○ **C.** lock
- ○ **D.** knob

1. sturdy table
   - ○ **A.** strong
   - ○ **B.** dining
   - ○ **C.** fragile
   - ○ **D.** chair

2. descend the staircase
   - ○ **A.** go down
   - ○ **B.** sweep
   - ○ **C.** hide
   - ○ **D.** climb up

3. nasty person
   - ○ **A.** pleasant
   - ○ **B.** mean
   - ○ **C.** wise
   - ○ **D.** human

4. widen the path
   - ○ **A.** enlarge
   - ○ **B.** trail
   - ○ **C.** hike
   - ○ **D.** narrow

5. hero's bravery
   - ○ **A.** courage
   - ○ **B.** cowardice
   - ○ **C.** wealth
   - ○ **D.** win

6. assist others
   - ○ **A.** help
   - ○ **B.** talk to
   - ○ **C.** ignore
   - ○ **D.** follow

7. brief recess
   - ○ **A.** fun
   - ○ **B.** boring
   - ○ **C.** short
   - ○ **D.** long

Reading Skills Practice Test 4

READING COMPREHENSION

Read each story. Then fill in the circle that best completes each sentence or answers each question.

SAMPLE

In 1998, Tom Whittaker made history. He became the first disabled person to climb Mount Everest. Ten years earlier, Tom had been in a car accident. He was badly **injured**. He lost both his right foot and his kneecap. Still, Tom wasn't going to let anything keep him from his goal. He was going to climb the world's tallest mountain.

I. In this passage, the word **injured** means
- ○ **A.** ignored.
- ○ **B.** annoyed.
- ○ **C.** shaken.
- ○ **D.** hurt.

2. This story is mainly about
- ○ **A.** how people avoid knee injuries.
- ○ **B.** why Mount Everest is too dangerous to climb.
- ○ **C.** a disabled person who climbed Mount Everest.
- ○ **D.** some very serious car accidents.

A. For most of us, headaches aren't a big deal. We get them now and then. They cause a little pain, then they go away. For about one in 10 people, however, headaches are more serious. They get extremely strong headaches called migraines.

Migraine headaches are more than just annoying. They can last for several hours, or even several days. Sometimes, people with migraines have so much pain that they have to stay in bed. They may not be able to do everyday activities. Often, they miss school or work. The problem is larger than you might think. Migraine headaches result in more than one million lost school days every year.

No one knows exactly what causes migraines. In different people, different things can set one off. With some people, eating certain foods can **trigger** a migraine. With others, it may be loud noises or blinking lights.

I. Compared to ordinary headaches, migraines are much
- ○ **A.** less serious.
- ○ **B.** less painful.
- ○ **C.** more painful.
- ○ **D.** more common.

2. In this story, the word **trigger** means
- ○ **A.** stop.
- ○ **B.** cause.
- ○ **C.** help.
- ○ **D.** slow down.

B.   Wilt Chamberlain was once basketball's greatest superstar. He played in the 1960s and 1970s. The big seven-foot center was a dazzling scorer. During his career, he had many excellent games. One game, however, stands out above the rest. That was the night he scored 100 points.

Why was the 100-point game so amazing? On most nights, it's not easy for a team to score that many points, let alone a player. Yet on March 2, 1962, Wilt did it all by himself. Wilt's team was the Philadelphia 76ers. The 76ers were playing against the New York Knicks. From the very beginning of the game, the 76ers gave the ball to Wilt. Almost every time they did so, Wilt managed to score. By halftime, Wilt had 41 points. After three quarters, he had 79 points. The fans went crazy as the game came to an end. Wilt had scored a record 100 points. This was the first time that it happened. It's never happened again.

I. What is the best title for this story?
  ○ **A.** "Wilt's 100-Point Game"
  ○ **B.** "The Philadelphia 76ers"
  ○ **C.** "How to Play Basketball"
  ○ **D.** "Isn't This Amazing?"

2. Which of these is an *opinion*?
  ○ **A.** Wilt played in the 1960s and 1970s.
  ○ **B.** Wilt was playing for the 76ers.
  ○ **C.** The 76ers were playing against New York.
  ○ **D.** Wilt was basketball's greatest superstar.

3. How many points did Wilt have at halftime?
  ○ **A.** 41
  ○ **B.** 79
  ○ **C.** 100
  ○ **D.** 141

C.   In the summer of 1997, a disaster struck Indonesia. The disaster was a series of fires that sent huge clouds of smoke rising into the air. The fires spread across a huge area. Thousands of acres were destroyed by flame. But it wasn't the flames that caused the most serious problems. It was the smoke. The smoke was so thick that it made people sick, even people hundreds of miles away.

The smoke swept over Indonesia. Then it spread to other countries. In Singapore and Malaysia, cities were choked by a thick layer of hazy smog. Millions of people suffered from the air pollution.

The thick smoke also caused accidents. Drivers could barely see the roads through their windshields. One airplane crashed in the haze. Two ships ran into each other in the sea. In November, rains came and put out the raging fires. By that time, tremendous damage had been done.

I. Where did the fires begin?
  ○ **A.** Malaysia.
  ○ **B.** Singapore.
  ○ **C.** Indonesia.
  ○ **D.** Indonesia and Singapore.

2. The two ships ran into each other because of
  ○ **A.** heavy rain.
  ○ **B.** thick smoke.
  ○ **C.** high waves.
  ○ **D.** hot flames.

3. The article's main purpose is to
  ○ **A.** explain how to put out forest fires.
  ○ **B.** tell you about a disaster in Indonesia.
  ○ **C.** persuade you not to start fires.
  ○ **D.** amuse you with a story about accidents.

D. All week long, I looked forward to finishing my book. The book was called *The Secret of the Hidden Cave*. It was a mystery, my favorite kind. Because I was busy with homework, I knew I wouldn't get the opportunity to finish it until Friday. Anyway, thinking about the story gave me something to look forward to. It was the most exciting book I had ever **encountered**.

When Friday came, I sat down on the couch and began to read. Each new page was better than the one before. What would the explorers find at the bottom of the cave? This question was driving me crazy! Finally, I got to the next-to-last page. I was about to learn the secret! When I turned the page, I was shocked. The last page was missing!

"It's not fair," I yelled. Then I heard a giggle. Looking into the next room, I saw my little sister. She was running away with something in her hand.

I. What is the best title for this story?
- ○ **A.** "The Mystery of the Missing Page"
- ○ **B.** "Why I Read Books"
- ○ **C.** "Too Much Homework"
- ○ **D.** "The Story of Famous Explorers"

2. In this story, the word **encountered** means
- ○ **A.** borrowed.   ○ **C.** finished.
- ○ **B.** returned.   ○ **D.** came across.

3. What can you guess from this story?
- ○ **A.** Mystery books are always missing a page.
- ○ **B.** The explorers found a skeleton in the cave.
- ○ **C.** The explorers didn't find anything in the cave.
- ○ **D.** The reader's sister tore out the last page.

E. August, 1999, was a sad month for the Russian space program. After 13½ years, it finally abandoned the space station *Mir*. The *Mir* had been in space since 1986. For years, it was the pride of the Russian program. Lately, however, the space station had been the scene of many accidents. Three occurred within a single year. First, a fire broke out on board. The crew of the *Mir* almost had to leave the space station. Then, a cargo ship crashed into the side of the space station. The crash caused major damage to the *Mir*'s solar panels. Finally, a computer breakdown nearly caused disaster.

In the end, none of these accidents caused the shutdown. The *Mir* was left behind because it was simply too old. The equipment was getting creaky. If astronauts stayed there, they would probably be risking their lives. The *Mir* had lasted far longer than expected. When it was built, the space station was supposed to last only five years.

I. Which of these is an *opinion*?
- ○ **A.** A cargo ship crashed into the space station.
- ○ **B.** The *Mir* had been in space since 1986.
- ○ **C.** August, 1999, was a sad month for the Russian space program.
- ○ **D.** A fire broke out on board.

2. What is the best title for this story?
- ○ **A.** "Lost in Space"
- ○ **B.** "A Safe Journey"
- ○ **C.** "The End of the *Mir*"
- ○ **D.** "All About Russia's Space Program"

3. The *Mir* closed down because
- ○ **A.** It was more than five years old.
- ○ **B.** The equipment was too old to be safe.
- ○ **C.** A computer broke down.
- ○ **D.** The astronaut's had been in space since 1986.

VOCABULARY

Synonyms

Read the underlined word in each phrase. Mark the word below it that has the same (or close to the same) meaning.

Sample:

take a <u>stroll</u>
- ○ **A.** look
- ○ **B.** number
- ○ **C.** board
- ○ **D.** walk

1. <u>squirming</u> around
- ○ **A.** standing
- ○ **B.** running
- ○ **C.** laughing
- ○ **D.** wriggling

2. nonstop <u>wailing</u>
- ○ **A.** crying
- ○ **B.** speaking
- ○ **C.** talking
- ○ **D.** joking

3. a surprising <u>triumph</u>
- ○ **A.** solution
- ○ **B.** victory
- ○ **C.** friend
- ○ **D.** day

4. <u>tattered</u> clothing
- ○ **A.** colorful
- ○ **B.** new
- ○ **C.** worn-out
- ○ **D.** clean

5. <u>waterfront</u> location
- ○ **A.** central
- ○ **B.** mountainous
- ○ **C.** island
- ○ **D.** shore

6. <u>sole</u> survivor
- ○ **A.** first
- ○ **B.** only
- ○ **C.** last
- ○ **D.** oldest

7. <u>tilt</u> your head
- ○ **A.** lean
- ○ **B.** nod
- ○ **C.** shake
- ○ **D.** lay

Antonyms

Read the underlined word in each phrase. Mark the word below it that means the opposite or nearly the opposite.

Sample:

<u>nervous</u> feeling
- ○ **A.** calm
- ○ **B.** frightened
- ○ **C.** angry
- ○ **D.** funny

1. <u>tighten</u> the hold
- ○ **A.** return
- ○ **B.** remove
- ○ **C.** slow down
- ○ **D.** loosen

2. <u>valuable</u> idea
- ○ **A.** useful
- ○ **B.** super
- ○ **C.** worthless
- ○ **D.** certain

3. possible <u>solution</u>
- ○ **A.** problem
- ○ **B.** surprise
- ○ **C.** activity
- ○ **D.** idea

4. <u>unfamiliar</u> faces
- ○ **A.** pleasant
- ○ **B.** known
- ○ **C.** beautiful
- ○ **D.** strange

5. <u>unfortunate</u> event
- ○ **A.** important
- ○ **B.** early
- ○ **C.** late
- ○ **D.** lucky

6 <u>tighten</u> your grip
- ○ **A.** brighten
- ○ **B.** loosen
- ○ **C.** increase
- ○ **D.** maintain

7. <u>spare</u> part
- ○ **A.** needed
- ○ **B.** extra
- ○ **C.** loose
- ○ **D.** costly

Reading Skills Practice Test 5

READING COMPREHENSION

Read each story. Then fill in the circle that best completes each sentence or answers each question.

Some kids in Japan may not have to feed the fish in their aquariums anymore. That's because they may choose to buy robotic fish instead. Robotic fish are little fish robots powered by light. The light causes the fish to move around inside the aquarium. A special design keeps the fish from bumping into the aquarium's walls.

I. A good title for this story would be
○ **A.** "New Aquariums."
○ **B.** "Robotic Fish."
○ **C.** "Pets in Japan."
○ **D.** "The Power of Light."

2. What causes the robotic fish to move?
○ **A.** light
○ **B.** fish food
○ **C.** robots
○ **D.** water

A.　Squeezed into a ship called the *Amistad*, the 53 slaves aboard could barely breathe. Each day, the crew gave them sips of water and scraps of food. The slaves were beaten and chained.

They had been kidnapped from Africa. On July 4, 1839, they broke free. They killed the captain and took control of *Amistad* off Cuba's coast, making the ship a famous symbol of freedom.

The *Amistad* story is famous for the rebellion and for what followed. After breaking free, the slaves tried to sail the ship back to their native Sierra Leone, in West Africa. The U.S. Navy captured the ship off the coast of Long Island and charged the slaves with murder.

In 1841, the U.S. Supreme Court ruled that the Africans had been illegally kidnapped. The Court allowed them to return to Africa.

I. What did the *Amistad* become a symbol of?
○ **A.** slavery
○ **B.** Africa
○ **C.** the Supreme Court
○ **D.** freedom

2. What happened after the U.S. Navy captured the ship?
○ **A.** The slaves were charged with murder.
○ **B.** The slaves were chained and beaten.
○ **C.** The slaves killed the ship's captain.
○ **D.** The slaves tried to sail to Sierra Leone.

3. The best title for this story is
○ **A.** "A History of Slavery."
○ **B.** "The Supreme Court."
○ **C.** "The Story of the *Amistad*."
○ **D.** "U.S. Navy Rescues."

B.   Now that the Summer Olympics are over, it's time to test your Australia awareness. Known as the "Land Down Under," Australia may be the world's most beautiful country. It's certainly the only country in the world that's both an island and a continent.

Want more Australia facts? It's about the size of the continental United States. Nineteen million people live there. Some of these people are Aborigines. Aborigines were Australia's first settlers, like Native Americans here in the U.S.

Australia is also home to some **unique** and interesting animals. Koala bears are one example. These picky eaters will only eat leaves from eucalyptus trees. They never drink water. Another famous Australian animal is the kangaroo. There are more kangaroos than people in Australia. A newborn kangaroo lives in its mother's pouch for as long as six months.

I.   Which of these is an *opinion*?
   ○ **A.** Australia may be the world's most beautiful country.
   ○ **B.** Australia is about the size of the continental United States.
   ○ **C.** Some Australians are Aborigines.
   ○ **D.** There are more kangaroos than people in Australia.

2.   Koala bears are picky eaters because
   ○ **A.** they never drink water.
   ○ **B.** they live in Australia.
   ○ **C.** they only eat kangaroos.
   ○ **D.** they only eat eucalyptus leaves.

3.   In this story, the word **unique** means
   ○ **A.** large.
   ○ **B.** small.
   ○ **C.** one-of-a-kind.
   ○ **D.** popular.

C.   Have you heard the buzz about bees? It's possible that the common honeybee can help scientists **detect** deadly land mines, or underground bombs.

Land mines kill more than 20,000 people each year. Soldiers bury the mines during wars, but the mines stay even after the wars have ended. People can't tell where land mines are until they explode.

Scientists are hoping that honeybees can help to find buried land mines and save people's lives.

How will it work? Honeybees' fuzzy bodies collect particles from the air, including particles from land mines. Scientists will use special sensors to check the bees for land mine particles. If they find some, the scientists can track the bees back to the mines and destroy them.

I.   In this story, the word **detect** means
   ○ **A.** kill.
   ○ **B.** find.
   ○ **C.** collect.
   ○ **D.** bury.

2.   According to the story, honeybees will
   ○ **A.** lead scientists to special sensors.
   ○ **B.** help lead scientists to land mines.
   ○ **C.** explode land mines.
   ○ **D.** sting the soldiers who bury land mines.

3.   Which is the best summary of this article?
   ○ **A.** Land mines are dangerous weapons that kill people.
   ○ **B.** No one can find land mines after soldiers bury them.
   ○ **C.** Honeybees have fuzzy bodies that collect particles from the air.
   ○ **D.** Honeybees may be able to help scientists detect land mines.

D. When Buddy Koerner eats an orange or a banana at school, he doesn't throw the peels into the trash. Buddy and his class have found a better use for fruit peels, limp lettuce, and soggy bread crusts. With the help of a few hundred worms, the class turns food scraps into a nourishing snack for planet Earth.

Each week, Buddy's class dumps food scraps into a special bin in their classroom. Red worms live inside the bin. They eat the scraps and make castings, or worm poop. The castings form compost, which looks like dark soil. Compost is rich in nutrients to help plants and lawns grow better.

Farmers have been making compost for at least 2,000 years. Today, more and more people are learning to compost in homes and schools. This kind of recycling can really help the planet.

1. Castings are
- ○ **A.** food scraps.
- ○ **B.** worms.
- ○ **C.** worm poop.
- ○ **D.** soil.

2. Buddy and his classmates make compost from
- ○ **A.** worms.
- ○ **B.** food scraps.
- ○ **C.** soil.
- ○ **D.** plants.

3. This story probably goes on to talk about
- ○ **A.** other kinds of worms.
- ○ **B.** other kinds of recycling.
- ○ **C.** what Buddy has for lunch every day.
- ○ **D.** the life cycle of worms.

E. Exercise helps to keep people healthy. But not everyone wants to play basketball or run marathons. Fortunately, there are plenty of other ways to get exercise. One good way is hiking.

What is hiking? Hiking really just means taking a long walk. Often, hiking involves going up or down a hill. Most people do it in the countryside, but you can also do it in town. And hiking doesn't really require any special equipment. All you need is a comfortable pair of shoes, a nutritious snack, and some water.

The shoes are very important. Uncomfortable hiking shoes can make walking painful. They can cause blisters or worse. It shouldn't hurt to hike, so wear sturdy, comfortable shoes.

The snack and water are also important. Hiking uses up the body's energy and fluids. A snack and some water can replace what you've lost. That means you'll be able to go up that one last hill.

1. If you hike in uncomfortable shoes you could
- ○ **A.** run out of energy.
- ○ **B.** get blisters.
- ○ **C.** fall down.
- ○ **D.** need more water.

2. What is the best title for this story?
- ○ **A.** "All Kinds of Exercise"
- ○ **B.** "A Guide to Hiking"
- ○ **C.** "The Importance of Shoes"
- ○ **D.** "Nutritious Snacks"

3. Which of these is not true about hiking?
- ○ **A.** It's like walking.
- ○ **B.** You can do it in the country.
- ○ **C.** You use a lot of special equipment.
- ○ **D.** It's important to take water on a hike.

VOCABULARY

Synonyms

Read the underlined word in each phrase. Mark the word below it that has the same (or close to the same) meaning.

Sample:

weary legs
- ○ **A.** tired
- ○ **B.** long
- ○ **C.** active
- ○ **D.** jumpy

---

1. unexpected defeat
   - ○ **A.** game
   - ○ **B.** number
   - ○ **C.** loss
   - ○ **D.** win

2. soaring through the air
   - ○ **A.** falling
   - ○ **B.** flying
   - ○ **C.** walking
   - ○ **D.** blowing

3. family tradition
   - ○ **A.** party
   - ○ **B.** gathering
   - ○ **C.** friend
   - ○ **D.** custom

4. fierce animal
   - ○ **A.** huge
   - ○ **B.** mean
   - ○ **C.** tiny
   - ○ **D.** hungry

5. weekly chore
   - ○ **A.** meal
   - ○ **B.** meeting
   - ○ **C.** party
   - ○ **D.** job

6. feeling uneasy
   - ○ **A.** unfit
   - ○ **B.** difficult
   - ○ **C.** disappointed
   - ○ **D.** uncomfortable

7. wring the wet clothes
   - ○ **A.** hang
   - ○ **B.** wash
   - ○ **C.** squeeze
   - ○ **D.** dry

Antonyms

Read the underlined word in each phrase. Mark the word below it that means the opposite or nearly the opposite.

Sample:

talk rapidly
- ○ **A.** quickly
- ○ **B.** slowly
- ○ **C.** funnily
- ○ **D.** normally

---

1. sure thing
   - ○ **A.** tiring
   - ○ **B.** uncertain
   - ○ **C.** new
   - ○ **D.** old

2. airplane takeoff
   - ○ **A.** wheel
   - ○ **B.** landing
   - ○ **C.** ticket
   - ○ **D.** flight

3. sloppy work
   - ○ **A.** neat
   - ○ **B.** good
   - ○ **C.** hard
   - ○ **D.** easy

4. back to reality
   - ○ **A.** life
   - ○ **B.** fantasy
   - ○ **C.** school
   - ○ **D.** work

5. thorough search
   - ○ **A.** incomplete
   - ○ **B.** neat
   - ○ **C.** incorrect
   - ○ **D.** successful

6. unseen problems
   - ○ **A.** unknown
   - ○ **B.** hard
   - ○ **C.** serious
   - ○ **D.** visible

7. valuable gift
   - ○ **A.** expensive
   - ○ **B.** birthday
   - ○ **C.** useless
   - ○ **D.** good

Reading Skills Practice Test 6

READING COMPREHENSION

Read each story. Then fill in the circle that best completes each sentence or answers each question.

Do you think you own the world's tiniest dog? *The Guinness Book of World Records* is the place to check! For 40 years, the *Guinness Book* has been **resolving** arguments about the biggest, the smallest, the fastest, and the strangest things in the world. Want to find out who blew the biggest bubble-gum bubble? Now you know where to look.

I. In this passage, the word **resolving** means
- ○ **A.** starting.
- ○ **B.** settling.
- ○ **C.** causing.
- ○ **D.** recording.

2. What is the best title for this passage?
- ○ **A.** "The World's Smallest Dog"
- ○ **B.** "Arguing for 40 Years"
- ○ **C.** "How to Blow a Giant Bubble"
- ○ **D.** "The Book With All the Records"

A.   One winter day, a young girl named Jenny was walking her dog named Hero. Jenny took Hero's tennis ball and threw it. "Rats!" she thought as the ball rolled onto the frozen pond. Hero ran out after it in a flash. "Hero!" Jenny screamed, running after her dog.

After about three large steps, the ice cracked under Jenny's feet and she fell into the pond. Hero ran to Jenny, but he fell in the water too. Jenny kept slipping as she tried to climb out. Meanwhile, Hero lifted his body up and slammed it down on the ice like a hammer until he made a path to the shore. That day Hero was a real hero.

I. What is the best title for this story?
- ○ **A.** "Hero Saves the Day "
- ○ **B.** "Recognizing Thin Ice"
- ○ **C.** "Favorite Pets"
- ○ **D.** "They Used to Play Fetch"

2. What can you guess from this story?
- ○ **A.** Hero hates the water.
- ○ **B.** Jenny can't swim.
- ○ **C.** Hero is a smart dog.
- ○ **D.** Jenny plays Little League baseball.

3. Why did Jenny go out on the ice?
- ○ **A.** to save Hero
- ○ **B.** to slide around on it
- ○ **C.** to see how strong it was
- ○ **D.** to play with Hero

B. It happened in 1947. For the first time, an African-American was stepping onto the field to play in a major-league baseball game. Jackie Robinson was playing for the Brooklyn Dodgers, the only team with enough courage to let this great athlete play. That day, baseball's color barrier was broken forever.

Despite the racism he met both on and off the field, Jackie was named Rookie of the Year and led the league in stolen bases. Two years later, he won the National League's Most Valuable Player (MVP) award. Robinson made it to the Baseball Hall of Fame in 1962.

Jackie changed baseball, but he also changed the way people thought. Civil rights leader Martin Luther King Jr. said, "Without Jackie Robinson, I could never have done what I did."

1. In 1947, Jackie Robinson
   ○ **A.** made the Baseball Hall of Fame.
   ○ **B.** was honored by Martin Luther King.
   ○ **C.** became the first African-American to play in the major leagues.
   ○ **D.** won the MVP award.

2. You can guess from this story that Robinson is most famous for
   ○ **A.** breaking baseball's color barrier.
   ○ **B.** leading the league in stolen bases.
   ○ **C.** playing for the Brooklyn Dodgers.
   ○ **D.** being named Rookie of the Year.

3. When did Robinson win the MVP award?
   ○ **A.** the year he joined the Dodgers
   ○ **B.** the year after he joined the Dodgers
   ○ **C.** two years after he joined the Dodgers
   ○ **D.** the year he made it to the Baseball Hall of Fame

C. Almost everyone likes bread. But not everyone knows how easy it is to make it. All you need are yeast, flour, and water.

First, mix a package of yeast with two cups of warm water. Let the mixture stand until bubbles form. Then start adding four cups of flour, a half a cup at a time. When the dough gets too thick to stir, scrape it onto a floured board and knead it. To knead, turn the dough in a circle and fold and punch it. Knead it for ten minutes as you add one more cup of flour. The dough is ready when it feels soft and smooth, not sticky.

After kneading, put the dough in a buttered bowl and cover it with a dish towel. Leave it there for an hour or more to rise. It should double in size. Then, knead it for another minute or so, and shape it into a loaf. Let it rise again for 45 minutes. Pop it in the oven to bake for 45 minutes in a 375-degree oven. When it's done, let it cool for ten minutes before slicing.

1. After the dough has doubled in size, you
   ○ **A.** knead it for ten minutes.
   ○ **B.** mix the yeast with two cups of water.
   ○ **C.** add flour a half a cup at a time.
   ○ **D.** knead it and shape it into a loaf.

2. The purpose of this article is to
   ○ **A.** teach you how to make bread.
   ○ **B.** tell you a funny cooking story.
   ○ **C.** persuade you to cook more.
   ○ **D.** make you like bread.

3. From this article, you can conclude that
   ○ **A.** bread requires many ingredients.
   ○ **B.** the author doesn't like bread.
   ○ **C.** making bread takes several hours.
   ○ **D.** dough is difficult to knead.

D. Put away those surfboards! Even the best surfer wouldn't want to ride a tsunami. The name tsunami comes from the Japanese language. It's the scientific term for a seismic sea wave, a giant wave caused by an undersea earthquake.

Scientists believe tsunamis occur when an earthquake lifts or tilts the ocean floor. The quake creates very long waves that speed across the sea. Tsunamis travel at up to 500 miles an hour. The waves grow in height as they reach the shore. Some monster-sized tsunamis can tower 60 feet or more above the ocean's surface.

Tsunamis are sometimes called tidal waves, but that name is misleading. High and low tides never cause tsunamis, only earthquakes or volcanic eruptions do. But by any name, tsunamis can be very dangerous. Hawaii has been hit by over 40 tsunamis!

I. What can cause a tsunami?
○ **A.** high and low tides
○ **B.** seismic sea waves
○ **C.** undersea earthquakes
○ **D.** scientific experiments

2. Which of these is an *opinion*?
○ **A.** Hawaii has been hit by over 40 tsunamis.
○ **B.** The best surfer wouldn't want to ride a tsunami.
○ **C.** Tsunamis grow in height as they reach the shore.
○ **D.** Tsunamis travel at up to 500 miles per hour.

3. This article would probably go on to talk about
○ **A.** destruction caused by tsunamis.
○ **B.** destruction caused by earthquakes.
○ **C.** surfers who like to ride tsunamis.
○ **D.** what causes high and low tides.

E. At 7:52 a.m. on May 20, 1927, Charles Lindbergh sat in the cockpit of his plane, the *Spirit of St. Louis*. The 25-year-old American was trying to fly nonstop across the Atlantic Ocean, from New York to Paris. The distance was 3,600 miles. No one had ever done this. If he made it, air travel would never be the same.

After taking off, Lindbergh had to find his way to Paris without the radar, radios, and computer equipment planes use today. Instead, he had a compass, maps, and the stars to help him find his way. Getting lost would be dangerous. He could easily run out of fuel before reaching land.

Finally, over 33 hours after he began his trip, Lindbergh landed in Paris. As he did, 25,000 people cheered. Lindbergh became an instant hero with a new nickname: the Lone Eagle.

I. How was Lindbergh's plane different from planes today?
○ **A.** It didn't have a name.
○ **B.** It had to take off and land on water.
○ **C.** It didn't have computer equipment.
○ **D.** It needed two people to fly it.

2. What is the best title for this story?
○ **A.** "The Next Plane to Paris"
○ **B.** "Pilots and Their Planes"
○ **C.** "A Trip Across the Atlantic"
○ **D.** "Lindbergh's Famous Flight"

3. Which of these is an *opinion*?
○ **A.** Lindbergh's plane was named the *Spirit of St. Louis*.
○ **B.** Lindbergh was the greatest pilot ever.
○ **C.** Lindbergh's trip took over 33 hours.
○ **D.** When he landed in Paris, 25,000 people cheered.

VOCABULARY

Synonyms

Read the underlined word in each phrase.
Mark the word below it that has the same
(or close to the same) meaning.

Sample:
abandon the ship
- ○ **A.** leave
- ○ **B.** sail
- ○ **C.** board
- ○ **D.** hide

I. narrow corridor
- ○ **A.** road
- ○ **B.** minded
- ○ **C.** door
- ○ **D.** hallway

2. riding solo
- ○ **A.** quickly
- ○ **B.** alone
- ○ **C.** carefully
- ○ **D.** fast

3. unique flavor
- ○ **A.** sweet
- ○ **B.** first-rate
- ○ **C.** one-of-a-kind
- ○ **D.** ordinary

4. soothe the pain
- ○ **A.** ignore
- ○ **B.** relieve
- ○ **C.** feel
- ○ **D.** worsen

5. unravel the mystery
- ○ **A.** solve
- ○ **B.** enjoy
- ○ **C.** forget
- ○ **D.** notice

6. possess a book
- ○ **A.** own
- ○ **B.** lend
- ○ **C.** carry
- ○ **D.** read

7. stale ideas
- ○ **A.** fresh
- ○ **B.** original
- ○ **C.** bad
- ○ **D.** old

Antonyms

Read the underlined word in each phrase.
Mark the word below it that means the
opposite or nearly the opposite.

Sample:
gush out of the tap
- ○ **A.** spill
- ○ **B.** trickle
- ○ **C.** topple
- ○ **D.** flow

I. confident character
- ○ **A.** funny
- ○ **B.** unsure
- ○ **C.** smug
- ○ **D.** pesky

2. gritty texture
- ○ **A.** smooth
- ○ **B.** stubby
- ○ **C.** tasty
- ○ **D.** bumpy

3. expand your horizons
- ○ **A.** visit
- ○ **B.** shrink
- ○ **C.** color
- ○ **D.** widen

4. an agreement between friends
- ○ **A.** apology
- ○ **B.** formula
- ○ **C.** contract
- ○ **D.** dispute

5. coastal highway
- ○ **A.** interstate
- ○ **B.** inland
- ○ **C.** frontier
- ○ **D.** circular

6. solemn occasion
- ○ **A.** frequent
- ○ **B.** rare
- ○ **C.** sorry
- ○ **D.** cheerful

7. elated look
- ○ **A.** happy
- ○ **B.** unsure
- ○ **C.** sad
- ○ **D.** pleased

Reading Skills Practice Test 7

READING COMPREHENSION

Read each story. Then fill in the circle that best completes each sentence or answers each question.

Since 1886, the Statue of Liberty has stood on Liberty Island in New York Bay. The beautiful statue was given to the United States by the people of France. With its torch raised high, the statue has welcomed immigrants from all over the world. It has become a **symbol** of American freedom.

1. What is the best title for this story?
- ○ **A.** "Immigrant Land"
- ○ **B.** "An American Symbol"
- ○ **C.** "Liberty Island"
- ○ **D.** "How a Statue Is Made"

2. In this story, the word **symbol** means
- ○ **A.** sculpture.
- ○ **B.** celebration.
- ○ **C.** sign.
- ○ **D.** warning.

A. Adobe is a Spanish word meaning "sun-dried brick." Adobe bricks are made by mixing sand, water, and small amounts of straw or grass. The mixture is then shaped into bricks, dried, and baked in the sun for about two weeks. Since sand is widely available in many deserts, desert dwellers have used adobe to make their homes for thousands of years.

1. The main idea of this story is that
- ○ **A.** adobe bricks are difficult to make.
- ○ **B.** deserts are hot.
- ○ **C.** people in deserts often build with adobe.
- ○ **D.** adobe is a Spanish word.

2. You would probably find this story in a book about
- ○ **A.** weather.
- ○ **B.** the sun.
- ○ **C.** building materials.
- ○ **D.** cactuses.

3. Which of these is an *opinion*?
- ○ **A.** Adobe is made from sand.
- ○ **B.** Adobe homes are beautiful
- ○ **C.** Adobe is a Spanish word.
- ○ **D.** Adobe is used in building.

B. Today, when you send a letter to a friend, it can get there in seconds—by electronic mail. However, centuries ago, sending a letter took much longer. About 2,400 years ago, a Persian king named Cyrus the Great **introduced** the first postal system. Messengers on horseback raced from station to station delivering letters. It took weeks or even months to receive a message from far away!

1. In this story, the word **introduced** means
○ **A.** met.
○ **B.** mailed.
○ **C.** used.
○ **D.** started.

2. The story would probably go on to talk about
○ **A.** other famous kings.
○ **B.** horses throughout history.
○ **C.** advances in sending mail.
○ **D.** the cost of stamps.

C. Scientists have been studying volcanoes for many years. They want to find ways to predict when volcanoes will erupt. Such knowledge could help protect people from a volcano's sudden burst of hot lava and ash. Although scientists can't say exactly when a volcano will erupt, they know that a slight change in the shape of the earth is one warning sign. Another is that some volcanoes emit a gas called sulfur dioxide before they erupt.

1. This story is mainly about
○ **A.** becoming a scientist.
○ **B.** natural disasters.
○ **C.** the dangers of volcanoes.
○ **D.** predicting volcanic eruptions.

2. You can guess that
○ **A.** scientists can predict all volcanic eruptions.
○ **B.** studying volcanoes is important.
○ **C.** volcanoes usually erupt in summer.
○ **D.** all volcanoes are tall.

D. As American pioneers headed west in the late 1700s and early 1800s, they used Conestoga wagons. These wagons were named for the valley in Pennsylvania where they were first built. Teams of four to six horses were used to **draw** the wagons. When it was hot or stormy, pioneers put canvas roofs on their wagons. When the pioneers came to rivers, they removed the vehicles' wide wheels, turning the wagons into boats!

1. Conestoga wagons were first made
○ **A.** in the West.
○ **B.** on the prairies.
○ **C.** in Pennsylvania.
○ **D.** in the 1800s.

2. In this story, the word **draw** means
○ **A.** run.
○ **B.** float.
○ **C.** paint.
○ **D.** pull.

3. Pioneers removed wagon wheels because
○ **A.** they had to cross rivers.
○ **B.** the wheels were broken.
○ **C.** the weather was stormy.
○ **D.** they wanted to sell them.

E. Have you ever used an encyclopedia? These reference books contain articles about many subjects. The articles are arranged in alphabetical order. To research a subject, follow these steps:

1. Find the encyclopedia index. It is usually in a separate volume. Use the index to find key words related to the subject you are researching.
2. Record from the index the names of articles related to your subject. Jot down the volume and page numbers so you can find the articles.
3. Using your list of articles, find the correct encyclopedia volumes. Then turn to the page on which each article begins.
4. Read each article. Write down the important information you want to remember.
5. Look at the end of the article for cross references. These references will send you to other articles related to your subject.

1. What is the best title for this story?
○ **A.** "Using an Encyclopedia"
○ **B.** "Taking Notes"
○ **C.** "Finding Cross References"
○ **D.** "Locating Subjects"

2. You can find cross references
○ **A.** in the front of each volume.
○ **B.** at the end of an article.
○ **C.** in your notes.
○ **D.** at the start of an article.

3. You can guess that encyclopedias
○ **A.** are useful research tools.
○ **B.** are just like dictionaries.
○ **C.** are difficult to use.
○ **D.** have very short articles.

4. What should you do right after you find the correct volume?
○ **A.** Find the index.
○ **B.** Take notes.
○ **C.** Look for cross references.
○ **D.** Find the article.

F. Dear Editor,

I am a fourth-grade student here in West Elmville. I am writing to respond to last week's article about school lunches. In the article, school officials said they planned to add more vegetables to the school lunch menu. That's a great idea. However, I would like to make a **recommendation**. Instead of adding more mushy canned veggies, our school cafeterias should have salad bars. A fresh salad is tasty and full of vitamins. And with a salad bar, kids can choose the veggies they like best.

Sincerely,
A Salad Fan

1. In this letter, the word **recommendation** means
○ **A.** meal.
○ **B.** suggestion.
○ **C.** vote.
○ **D.** addition.

2. You would probably see this letter
○ **A.** in a local newspaper.
○ **B.** on a school principal's desk.
○ **C.** in your mailbox.
○ **D.** in a book about nutrition.

3. The author wrote this letter to
○ **A.** get a job in a cafeteria.
○ **B.** share his or her opinion.
○ **C.** entertain readers.
○ **D.** tell how to grow fresh vegetables.

VOCABULARY

Synonyms

Read the underlined word in each phrase. Mark the word below it that has the same (or close to the same) meaning.

Sample:

massive creature
- ○ **A.** huge
- ○ **B.** quiet
- ○ **C.** hungry
- ○ **D.** ugly

I. link together
- ○ **A.** key
- ○ **B.** connect
- ○ **C.** blast
- ○ **D.** walk

2. important mission
- ○ **A.** secret
- ○ **B.** day
- ○ **C.** task
- ○ **D.** title

3. humorous story
- ○ **A.** long
- ○ **B.** funny
- ○ **C.** short
- ○ **D.** sad

4. purchase goods
- ○ **A.** clean
- ○ **B.** paint
- ○ **C.** sell
- ○ **D.** buy

5. heavy parcel
- ○ **A.** weight
- ○ **B.** rain
- ○ **C.** light
- ○ **D.** package

6. cautious driver
- ○ **A.** fast
- ○ **B.** careful
- ○ **C.** unsafe
- ○ **D.** taxi

7. conceal a smile
- ○ **A.** hide
- ○ **B.** draw
- ○ **C.** reveal
- ○ **D.** force

Multiple Meanings

Read each set of sentences. Mark the word that makes sense in both sentences.

Sample:

The doctor said her _____ had a stomach flu.
Be _____ while others at the table finish eating.
- ○ **A.** son
- ○ **B.** staff
- ○ **C.** patient
- ○ **D.** kind

I. Wheat and corn are both examples of _____.
I found a few _____ of sand in my shoe.
- ○ **A.** plants
- ○ **B.** grains
- ○ **C.** foods
- ○ **D.** pieces

2. He works the early _____ at the library.
Mary had to _____ her chair to get a better view.
- ○ **A.** job
- ○ **B.** turn
- ○ **C.** move
- ○ **D.** shift

3. The family bought a _____ of farmland.
Did you enjoy that book's exciting _____?
- ○ **A.** piece
- ○ **B.** plot
- ○ **C.** mile
- ○ **D.** hero

4. The baby can't walk, but she _____ along the floor.
The scary movie gave me the _____.
- ○ **A.** creeps
- ○ **B.** moves
- ○ **C.** slithers
- ○ **D.** crawls

Reading Skills Practice Test 8

READING COMPREHENSION

Read each story. Then fill in the circle that best completes each sentence or answers each question.

SAMPLE

American girls are shooting pucks and scoring goals all over the U.S. They are skating their way into a sport once thought to be just for boys. Since 1992, the number of American girls playing in organized ice-hockey leagues has **increased** from 5,500 to more than 20,000.

1. What is the main idea of this story?
- A. Ice hockey is a dangerous sport.
- B. Many girls play ice hockey now.
- C. Only boys should play hockey.
- D. Only girls should play hockey.

2. In this story, the word **increased** means
- A. gone up.
- B. skated.
- C. fallen.
- D. gone down.

A. The next time you pick up a bag of potato chips, read the label. You might notice a new ingredient—Olestra. Olestra was invented as a **substitute** for ingredients that are high in fat, such as butter or oil. But unlike butter and oil, Olestra doesn't add fat or calories to foods. That's because Olestra is not a food. It just passes through the body, without being digested.

Some people say that snacks containing Olestra taste as delicious as the real things. But Olestra can cause stomach cramps and other side effects. "I would rather see kids eat healthy snacks rather than potato chips," says diet expert Jodie Shield. "That's a better goal than choosing Olestra chips over regular high-fat chips."

1. What is the best title for this story?
- A. "Everyone Loves Potato Chips"
- B. "Olestra Tastes Great"
- C. "Olestra May Not Be the Answer"
- D. "How to Improve Your Diet"

2. In this story, the word **substitute** means
- A. greasy.
- B. replacement.
- C. addition.
- D. subtraction.

3. Which is an *opinion* about Olestra?
- A. It tastes delicious.
- B. It isn't digested by the body.
- C. It can be used in snack foods.
- D. It may cause stomach cramps.

4. Olestra can be used to make foods
- A. taste better.
- B. saltier.
- C. lower in fat.
- D. lower in cost.

B. The state of Connecticut used to have one official hero—a man named Nathan Hale. But in 1993, a fourth-grade class from New Canaan Country School decided that their state should have a female hero too. So the students began researching important women in Connecticut's history. They chose Prudence Crandall, a teacher who had let black students attend her school—even though it was against the law—back in 1832. Eventually, Crandall went to jail for her efforts. After the students chose Crandall, they asked lawmakers to introduce a bill recognizing her as a hero. That bill was made a law in 1995.

1. Prudence Crandall was a teacher in
○ **A.** 1993.   ○ **C.** 1832.
○ **B.** 1995.   ○ **D.** 1997.

2. Which happened last?
○ **A.** Crandall became a state hero.
○ **B.** Crandall went to jail.
○ **C.** The students chose Crandall.
○ **D.** Crandall let black students go to her school.

3. From this story, you can guess that
○ **A.** the fourth-graders went to jail.
○ **B.** Nathan Hale is no longer a hero.
○ **C.** only men can be heroes.
○ **D.** women probably aren't recognized as heroes as often as they could be.

C.   November 20, 1997
Dear Principal,
        I think the students at our school should wear uniforms. Many schools already have them. Uniforms will help our families save money, since we would have to **purchase** only one or two uniforms for the whole year. Uniforms could also give us more pride in our school. And best of all, if we all wore uniforms, kids wouldn't tease each other about their clothes.
        I know some students think uniforms are ugly and uncomfortable. But maybe we can pick a uniform that everyone likes. I think this is a terrific idea for our school.

                Sincerely,
                Justin Jones

1. This letter was written by
○ **A.** a father.
○ **B.** a mother.
○ **C.** a teacher.
○ **D.** a student.

2. In this letter, the word **purchase** means
○ **A.** wear.   ○ **C.** buy.
○ **B.** see.   ○ **D.** sell.

3. Which of these is a *fact* about uniforms?
○ **A.** They are uncomfortable.
○ **B.** Some schools already have them.
○ **C.** They are ugly.
○ **D.** They aren't too expensive.

4. Justin wrote this letter to
○ **A.** ask for new clothes.
○ **B.** apologize to the principal.
○ **C.** suggest that students wear uniforms.
○ **D.** thank the principal.

5. Some students don't want to wear uniforms because they think
○ **A.** uniforms are expensive.
○ **B.** school pride is silly.
○ **C.** the principal is mean.
○ **D.** uniforms can be ugly and uncomfortable.

D. Zoom! Each spring, dozens of cars race from New York City to Washington, D.C.—without using a single drop of gas! These cars run on electricity.

Most cars run on gasoline. When cars burn this fuel, they pollute the air with smelly exhaust. Electric cars run on batteries. Since they don't burn fuel, they produce much less pollution.

Events, like this 310-mile race, give electric carmakers a chance to show off their **vehicles**. They hope to convince people that electric cars are the wave of the future. But so far, electric cars can travel only about 40 miles on one charge of electricity. A gasoline-powered car could probably go about 200 miles on one tank of gas. That means electric cars require five times as many pit stops—and that may be the reason that these cars haven't caught on yet.

I. What is the main idea of this article?
○ **A.** Gasoline is an expensive fuel.
○ **B.** Electric-car races are exciting.
○ **C.** Everyone wants an electric car.
○ **D.** The electric car is a clean, if slow, way to travel.

2. In this article, the word **vehicles** means
○ **A.** cars.   ○ **C.** speed.
○ **B.** gasoline.   ○ **D.** tires.

3. Cars produce smelly exhaust when they
○ **A.** recharge.   ○ **C.** burn gasoline.
○ **B.** speed.   ○ **D.** use batteries.

4. The next paragraph might talk about
○ **A.** monster trucks.
○ **B.** other ways to cut down on car pollution.
○ **C.** other uses of electricity.
○ **D.** famous race-car drivers.

E. Many years ago in Greece, there lived a king named Midas. He wished for the power to turn things to gold simply by touching them. Since Midas was a good king, a god named Dionysus granted his wish. Shouting with joy, Midas ran through his palace, touching everything. And everything he owned became gold. He was rich beyond his wildest dreams.

At dinner time, King Midas reached for some bread, and the bread turned to gold. He reached for some water, and his lips turned the water to gold. King Midas realized he would soon die of hunger or thirst. Weeping gold tears, he went to the god Dionysus and begged the god to remove the golden touch.

"You have been greedy and foolish," scolded Dionysus. But he took pity on Midas, and sent the king to a special river to wash his hands. Midas did so, and the golden touch was washed away.

I. This story is mainly about
○ **A.** how Midas got to be very rich.
○ **B.** how Midas learned a lesson about being greedy.
○ **C.** how Dionysus played a mean trick.
○ **D.** how to cook gold food.

2. Midas got rid of the golden touch by
○ **A.** eating bread and water.
○ **B.** washing his hands in a fountain.
○ **C.** sleeping in a special bed.
○ **D.** washing his hands in a special river.

3. This story teaches that
○ **A.** all wishes are foolish.
○ **B.** some things are more important than gold.
○ **C.** some rivers are cleaner than others.
○ **D.** Greek gods should feel sorry for kings who love gold.

VOCABULARY

Synonyms

Read the underlined word in each phrase. Mark the word below it that has the same (or close to the same) meaning.

Sample:

injure your foot
- ○ **A.** hurt
- ○ **B.** kill
- ○ **C.** toe
- ○ **D.** tickle

1. holler loudly
   - ○ **A.** noisy
   - ○ **B.** whisper
   - ○ **C.** shout
   - ○ **D.** laugh

2. take a ferry
   - ○ **A.** car
   - ○ **B.** boat
   - ○ **C.** grab
   - ○ **D.** taxi

3. faithful dog
   - ○ **A.** brown
   - ○ **B.** furry
   - ○ **C.** collar
   - ○ **D.** loyal

4. bewildered student
   - ○ **A.** smart
   - ○ **B.** book
   - ○ **C.** confused
   - ○ **D.** teacher

5. solid foundation
   - ○ **A.** base
   - ○ **B.** rock
   - ○ **C.** roof
   - ○ **D.** hard

6. essential equipment
   - ○ **A.** necessary
   - ○ **B.** expensive
   - ○ **C.** cheap
   - ○ **D.** sturdy

7. rigid material
   - ○ **A.** stiff
   - ○ **B.** red
   - ○ **C.** natural
   - ○ **D.** soft

Antonyms

Read the underlined word in each phrase. Mark the word below it that means the opposite or nearly the opposite.

Sample:

felt sorrow
- ○ **A.** silly
- ○ **B.** joy
- ○ **C.** saw
- ○ **D.** sadness

1. brief message
   - ○ **A.** short
   - ○ **B.** long
   - ○ **C.** note
   - ○ **D.** funny

2. the nearest exit
   - ○ **A.** entrance
   - ○ **B.** slow
   - ○ **C.** door
   - ○ **D.** leave

3. a harmless spider
   - ○ **A.** safe
   - ○ **B.** ugly
   - ○ **C.** hairy
   - ○ **D.** poisonous

4. a harsh sound
   - ○ **A.** gentle
   - ○ **B.** scream
   - ○ **C.** noise
   - ○ **D.** alarm

5. visit frequently
   - ○ **A.** often
   - ○ **B.** travel
   - ○ **C.** rarely
   - ○ **D.** gladly

6. efficient worker
   - ○ **A.** busy
   - ○ **B.** hard
   - ○ **C.** wasteful
   - ○ **D.** careful

7. defiant attitude
   - ○ **A.** unhappy
   - ○ **B.** respectful
   - ○ **C.** confused
   - ○ **D.** poor

Reading Skills Practice Test 9

READING COMPREHENSION

Read each story. Then fill in the circle that best completes each sentence or answers each question.

SAMPLE

More hurricanes happen in September than in any other month. Why? In the late summer and early fall, ocean water is warm after a summer in the sun. The warm, **moist** air rises off the surface of the ocean and forms thunderstorms. The thunderstorms can spin into powerful hurricanes.

1. What is the best title for this story?
- ○ **A.** "Why Hurricanes Are So Powerful"
- ○ **B.** "Why Hurricanes Often Happen in September"
- ○ **C.** "Why the Ocean Is Warm in September"
- ○ **D.** "Why Late Summer and Early Fall Are Great Seasons"

2. In this story, the word **moist** means
- ○ **A.** makes.
- ○ **B.** wet.
- ○ **C.** stops.
- ○ **D.** hides.

A. Kids at Dupuy Elementary school in Birmingham, Alabama, study more than reading, writing, and math. They also take classes in manners! They practice when to say "please" and "thank you" and learn the polite way to pass food at the lunch table.

They also learn to eat with a fork, not fingers; to say "hello" and not "yo" when they answer the phone; to shake hands when meeting someone—especially a grown-up; not to interrupt when others are speaking; and to say "excuse me" instead of pushing.

1. This story is mostly about
- ○ **A.** how to pass food at the lunch table.
- ○ **B.** a school's classes in manners.
- ○ **C.** why Alabama students are so polite.
- ○ **D.** how one school teaches reading, writing, and math.

2. At Dupuy Elementary school, kids learn the polite way to
- ○ **A.** study math.
- ○ **B.** interrupt when others are speaking.
- ○ **C.** pass food at the lunch table.
- ○ **D.** pass food on the school bus.

3. Which of the following statements is an *opinion*?
- ○ **A.** More schools should teach classes in manners.
- ○ **B.** Dupuy Elementary school teaches classes in manners.
- ○ **C.** Many schools don't teach classes in manners.
- ○ **D.** Dupuy's classes teach kids to shake hands when meeting someone.

B.   When people think about wildlife, they often think about fields and forests. But many wild animals live in cities. One creature often found in city skies is the peregrine falcon.

     In the wilderness, peregrine falcons make their homes on steep, rocky cliffs. In cities, these birds nest on skyscrapers. Peregrine falcons like to be high in the sky so they can spot their favorite food—pigeons. Then the falcons swoop down and snatch their **prey** right out of the sky!

     So if you live in a city and you see something whiz by faster than 200 miles per hour, it may not be a jet plane. It may be a peregrine falcon—the fastest flying animal alive!

I. In this story, the word **prey** means an animal that
○ **A.** can fly.   ○ **B.** is hunted.
○ **C.** has wings.   ○ **D.** lives in cities.

2. A peregrine falcon can fly faster than
○ **A.** 2,000 miles per hour.
○ **B.** a jet plane.
○ **C.** a few other flying animals.
○ **D.** 200 miles per hour.

3. From this story, you can guess that
○ **A.** peregrine falcons eat nothing but pigeons.
○ **B.** peregrine falcons build huge nests.
○ **C.** peregrine falcons live both in cities and in the wilderness.
○ **D.** peregrine falcons live only in cities.

C.   If you're a kid under 18, and you live in New Orleans, Louisiana, you can't be out on the street on a school night after 8 p.m. If you are under 16 and you want to visit the country's largest mall—the Mall of America in Bloomington, Minnesota—on a Friday or Saturday night, you have to be with your mom or dad, or another grown-up.

     Rules like these are called curfews. They prevent people from traveling freely, usually after dark. In many places, curfews are a cause of debate. Many people think curfews are a good way to **reduce** crimes committed by young people. They say curfews make communities safer. But other people say curfews are unfair because they punish all kids for the behavior of a few troublemakers.

I. In this story, the word **reduce** means
○ **A.** make more.
○ **B.** stop totally.
○ **C.** make fewer.
○ **D.** spread.

2. In New Orleans, kids under 18 can't be out on the streets after 8 p.m.
○ **A.** on any night.
○ **B.** on school nights.
○ **C.** on Fridays and Saturdays.
○ **D.** near the mall.

3. The story tells
○ **A.** why the Mall of America is a safe place to visit.
○ **B.** why most people want curfews in their communities.
○ **C.** why most people think curfews are unfair.
○ **D.** why people disagree about curfews.

4. Which of these is a *fact* about curfews?
○ **A.** They are unfair to kids.
○ **B.** They prevent people from traveling freely.
○ **C.** They always make communities safer.
○ **D.** The city of New Orleans is lucky to have one.

D.   If you saw Stan Herd at work, you'd probably think that he looked like an ordinary farmer. And most of the **materials** he works with—like seeds, soil, and a tractor—are just ordinary farm items. But in one very big way, Stan has little in common with other farmers. Stan Herd doesn't just plant crops, he's a crop artist! Stan plants and shapes crops into pictures so huge you need to view them from an airplane.

Many of Stan's pictures are modeled after famous works of art. For example, he once planted 20 acres of crops in the shape of Vincent van Gogh's painting "Sunflowers." Naturally, Stan used real sunflowers

Stan does most of his work on his farm in Kansas. But recently, he traveled to New York City to plant a landscape along the East River. No need for an airplane in the city—you can see Stan's work from nearby skyscrapers!

1. What is the main idea of this story?
- ○ **A.** Stan Herd is a better artist than Vincent van Gogh.
- ○ **B.** Stan Herd uses some very strange materials on his farm.
- ○ **C.** Stan Herd's art is so big, you must view it from an airplane.
- ○ **D.** Stan Herd is not just a farmer, he's a crop artist.

2. In this story, the word **materials** means
- ○ **A.** tools.
- ○ **C.** fabrics.
- ○ **B.** crops.
- ○ **D.** tractor.

3. In this story, where did Stan Herd plant a landscape?
- ○ **A.** along the East River in Kansas.
- ○ **B.** on top of a skyscraper in New York City
- ○ **C.** along the East River in New York City
- ○ **D.** near the Kansas River

E.   One day the sun and the wind had an argument. The wind claimed that he was stronger than the sun. "Wrong," replied the sun. "I am stronger than you."

As they were disputing, a woman came down the road, wearing a heavy woolen coat.

"Here's how we can decide who is stronger," shouted the wind. "See that woman. Let's see which of us can remove her coat."

"Good idea," the sun replied. "You go first." So the wind started to blow. He blew and blew, as hard as he could. Trees swayed almost to the ground, but the woman only wrapped her coat more tightly around her.

Now the sun began to shine. She shone down on the woman, until the woman grew warm and unbuttoned her coat. The sun kept on shining. Soon, the woman removed her coat and laid it over her arm.

"Alas, you win," said the wind to the sun. "Your gentleness has succeeded where my rudeness failed."

1. This story is mainly about
- ○ **A.** solar power.
- ○ **B.** how the wind beat the sun in a contest.
- ○ **C.** how the wind learned a lesson from the sun.
- ○ **D.** why we don't wear coats when it's warm out.

2. The woman removed her coat because
- ○ **A.** the wind was blowing it off.
- ○ **B.** she became too warm in the sun.
- ○ **C.** she wanted the wind to lose the contest.
- ○ **D.** she didn't like the coat.

3. This story teaches that
- ○ **A.** you shouldn't wear a coat in warm weather.
- ○ **B.** the wind shouldn't blow so hard.
- ○ **C.** bullies often get their way.
- ○ **D.** kindness may get you further than rudeness.

VOCABULARY

Synonyms

Read the underlined word in each phrase. Mark the word below it that has the same (or close to the same) meaning.

Sample:

annoy your brother
- A. help
- C. sister
- B. bother
- D. please

1. summer drought
   - A. dry spell
   - C. winter
   - B. rainy season
   - D. sunshine

2. brief lesson
   - A. long
   - C. teacher
   - B. tennis
   - D. short

3. strong ability
   - A. smell
   - C. skill
   - B. muscle
   - D. weakness

4. hastily finished
   - A. quickly
   - C. purple
   - B. completed
   - D. slowly

5. soar through the sky
   - A. run
   - C. float
   - B. fly
   - D. cloud

6. became hysterical
   - A. emotional
   - C. tired
   - B. calm
   - D. energetic

7. elevate the temperature
   - A. read
   - C. describe
   - B. criticize
   - D. raise

Antonyms

Read the underlined word in each phrase. Mark the word below it that means the opposite or nearly the opposite.

Sample:

grandmother's kindness
- A. age
- C. meanness
- B. grandchild
- D. happiness

1. fortunate event
   - A. unlucky
   - C. happening
   - B. lucky
   - D. exciting

2. student's failure
   - A. books
   - C. problem
   - B. teacher
   - D. success

3. friendly youngster
   - A. adult
   - C. child
   - B. puppy
   - D. rude

4. amuse the child
   - A. bore
   - C. watch
   - B. scare
   - D. entertain

5. fled the disaster
   - A. ran to
   - C. ran from
   - B. caused
   - D. tragedy

6. an earned privilege
   - A. punishment
   - C. treat
   - B. paycheck
   - D. position

7. the courage to persist
   - A. speak
   - C. continue
   - B. act
   - D. quit

Reading Skills Practice Test 10

READING COMPREHENSION

Read each story. Then fill in the circle that best completes each sentence or answers each question.

For centuries, humans have lived in cities. People came to cities to trade goods, to find jobs, and to be near other people. Today, however, experts are asking if cities are still **necessary**. E-mail and the Internet have changed the way people live. They can work from their homes, even if their homes are far from any town. They can shop over the Internet. They can even use the Internet to talk with friends.

1. In this passage, the word **necessary** means
○ **A.** growing.
○ **B.** fun.
○ **C.** needed.
○ **D.** uncertain.

2. This story is mainly about
○ **A.** how to work in a city.
○ **B.** how people talk with friends.
○ **C.** whether or not people still need cities.
○ **D.** what is was like to live in old cities

A. Are you tired of plain-old apples and oranges? Add some spice to your diet by trying tropical fruit! If you look around the supermarket, you'll find flavorful items to give your lunch a whole new twist. Here are some possibilities:

Try a mango. You may already be familiar with mango-flavored food, like candy or ice cream. There's nothing quite like a real mango, however. A fresh ripe mango has sweet orange meat. It's the perfect snack in summer.

There's also the star fruit. Shaped like its name, the star fruit is a special crunchy treat.

The pomelo is another idea. Pomelos are like large grapefruits, but sweeter and drier. Since they don't have too much juice, they're a great fruit to eat when you don't want to get your hands sticky.

If none of these interest you, here are some more **suggestions**: papayas, kumquats, cherimoyas, lychees, or mangosteens.

1. Compared to pomelos, grapefruits are
○ **A.** crunchier.
○ **B.** less sweet.
○ **C.** less juicy.
○ **D.** larger.

2. In this story, the word **suggestions** means
○ **A.** answers.
○ **B.** flavors.
○ **C.** ideas.
○ **D.** vegetables.

B. This was a big year for zoos! Many of them opened new attractions.

The San Diego Zoo is famous. Now there's a new reason to visit. It's called Ituri Forest. The forest is modeled after an African river basin. Visitors can watch swimming hippos, otters, and buffalo.

In Philadelphia, the zookeepers built a new home for the gorillas. The gorillas have to share their house. Eleven kinds of animals live there.

The Dallas Zoo was very busy. For starters, they opened the Endangered Tiger area. Tigers roam through an actual rain forest. It's the best place to see big cats. They also have a new hospital. It's 20 times bigger than the old one. It has lots of space to help sick animals.

I. What is the best title for this story?
- ○ **A.** "Zoos Get Better"
- ○ **B.** "See the Swimming Hippos"
- ○ **C.** "Tigers in the Zoo"
- ○ **D.** "The Dallas Zoo Hospital"

2. Which of these is an *opinion*?
- ○ **A.** Visitors can watch swimming hippos.
- ○ **B.** It's 20 times bigger than the old one.
- ○ **C.** It's the best place to see big cats.
- ○ **D.** The Dallas Zoo opened an Endangered Tiger area.

3. Where can a visitor see tigers roam?
- ○ **A.** The Philadelphia Zoo
- ○ **B.** The Dallas Zoo
- ○ **C.** The San Diego Zoo
- ○ **D.** Ituri Forest

C. Is there life on other planets? Some scientists think so. They don't expect to find human-like creatures or little green men. If life exists, it's probably tiny bacteria. Discoveries here on Earth have shaped this thinking.

For a long time, scientists thought other planets were too cold for life. Now they've changed their minds. It's because of studies done near the South Pole, one of the coldest places on Earth. They've found bacteria that live in the ice. The bacteria survive in tiny pockets of water.

If there's life near the South Pole, there may be life on cold planets. Mars is one possibility. Europa, a moon of Jupiter, is another. Europa is covered with ice. Beneath the ice, there may be an ocean. Scientists say that this water may support life.

I. Which is the best summary of this article?
- ○ **A.** Scientists have been studying the South Pole.
- ○ **B.** Life is found on Mars and Europa.
- ○ **C.** Scientists think there may be life on other planets.
- ○ **D.** Europa, an icy moon, may be covered in water.

2. Scientists used to believe that
- ○ **A.** cold planets could not support life.
- ○ **B.** little green men lived on other planets.
- ○ **C.** life could be found on Europa.
- ○ **D.** life could be found on Mars.

3. Scientists changed their mind about life on other planets because
- ○ **A.** Mars and Europa are not very cold.
- ○ **B.** of voyages to other planets.
- ○ **C.** of studies done here on Earth.
- ○ **D.** Jupiter's moon is covered in ice.

D. "Take your rain gear," Sarah's mom said as Sarah ran out the door to catch her ride. "Don't need it," Sarah yelled back. "It's a beautiful day."

In fact, it was a little bit cloudy, but the sun was out. The nature walk was only supposed to take two hours. Sarah was sure that the weather wouldn't change that quickly. As Sarah and her troop walked through the woods, the sky **became** dark and gray. As they marched up the hill toward Skinner's Lake, the wind howled. "I'm glad I brought my poncho," said Shawn. "You never know around here; the weather can change in a second."

Sarah glared at him. "What do you know? It's a beautiful day, Shawn."

"I agree," he replied. "A beautiful day for a thunderstorm."

I. How does Sarah seem to feel toward Shawn?
- ○ **A.** friendly
- ○ **B.** annoyed
- ○ **C.** worried about
- ○ **D.** sorry for

2. In this story, the word **became** means
- ○ **A.** grew.
- ○ **B.** felt.
- ○ **C.** sounded.
- ○ **D.** was no longer.

3. This story probably goes on to talk about
- ○ **A.** what Sarah and Shawn ate for lunch.
- ○ **B.** other nature hikes the troop had taken.
- ○ **C.** different kinds of insects found in the forest.
- ○ **D.** whether or not it rained.

E. People in the United States love their ice cream. The average American eats about 47 pints each year. That's almost two hundred scoops of the frozen stuff! There's no doubt about it. We're the biggest ice cream eaters in the world! Who's next? Believe it or not, New Zealand. New Zealanders **consume** about 40 pints a year. Australians are in third place at 32 pints each.

You might think that Canadians would be big ice cream eaters. After all, Canada is right next to the United States. The average Canadian, however, only eats 27 pints. Maybe it's just too cold in Canada to eat that much ice cream.

The top-selling flavor is vanilla. Some call it boring, but people seem to eat it up. Believe it or not, chocolate is only the fifth favorite flavor. It trails fruit flavors, nut flavors, and candy-mix flavors in popularity.

I. Which of these is an *opinion*?
- ○ **A.** New Zealanders eat 40 pints a year.
- ○ **B.** Canadians eat 27 pints a year.
- ○ **C.** It's too cold to eat ice cream in Canada.
- ○ **D.** The top-selling flavor is vanilla.

2. What is the best title for this story?
- ○ **A.** "Ice Cream Facts and Figures"
- ○ **B.** "Chocolate Ice Cream"
- ○ **C.** "New Zealand Takes Second Place in Ice Cream Race"
- ○ **D.** "How Much Is a Pint?"

3. After the United States and New Zealand, which country eats the most ice cream?
- ○ **A.** Canada
- ○ **B.** Australia
- ○ **C.** France
- ○ **D.** Sweden

4. In this story, the word **consume** means
- ○ **A.** melt.
- ○ **B.** eat.
- ○ **C.** make.
- ○ **D.** borrow.

VOCABULARY

Synonyms

Read the underlined word in each phrase. Mark the word below it that has the same (or close to the same) meaning.

Sample:

weary legs
- ○ **A.** tired
- ○ **B.** long
- ○ **C.** active
- ○ **D.** jumpy

1. unexpected victory
   - ○ **A.** game
   - ○ **B.** number
   - ○ **C.** loss
   - ○ **D.** win

2. soaring through the air
   - ○ **A.** falling
   - ○ **B.** flying
   - ○ **C.** walking
   - ○ **D.** blowing

3. family tradition
   - ○ **A.** party
   - ○ **B.** gathering
   - ○ **C.** friend
   - ○ **D.** custom

4. giant animal
   - ○ **A.** fierce
   - ○ **B.** huge
   - ○ **C.** tiny
   - ○ **D.** hungry

5. early sunset
   - ○ **A.** meltdown
   - ○ **B.** suntan
   - ○ **C.** sunrise
   - ○ **D.** sundown

6. a vague idea
   - ○ **A.** bad
   - ○ **B.** unclear
   - ○ **C.** near
   - ○ **D.** great

7. an outlandish outfit
   - ○ **A.** outgrown
   - ○ **B.** handsome
   - ○ **C.** silly
   - ○ **D.** common

Antonyms

Read the underlined word in each phrase. Mark the word below it that means the opposite or nearly the opposite.

Sample:

walking steadily
- ○ **A.** unevenly
- ○ **B.** quickly
- ○ **C.** slowly
- ○ **D.** normally

1. sure thing
   - ○ **A.** tiring
   - ○ **B.** uncertain
   - ○ **C.** new
   - ○ **D.** old

2. airplane takeoff
   - ○ **A.** wheel
   - ○ **B.** landing
   - ○ **C.** ticket
   - ○ **D.** flight

3. pleased to meet you
   - ○ **A.** lucky
   - ○ **B.** surprised
   - ○ **C.** happy
   - ○ **D.** unhappy

4. wicked ways
   - ○ **A.** good
   - ○ **B.** smart
   - ○ **C.** stout
   - ○ **D.** awful

5. thorough search
   - ○ **A.** incomplete
   - ○ **B.** neat
   - ○ **C.** incorrect
   - ○ **D.** successful

6. renew the friendship
   - ○ **A.** end
   - ○ **B.** begin
   - ○ **C.** enjoy
   - ○ **D.** abuse

7. decline the offer
   - ○ **A.** ignore
   - ○ **B.** accept
   - ○ **C.** debate
   - ○ **D.** consider

Reading Skills Practice Test II

READING COMPREHENSION

Read each story. Then fill in the circle that best completes each sentence or answers each question.

Are you letting too much water go down the drain in your house? We all know that it's important not to waste water. But most of us use a lot more water than we think. Try these two simple ways to cut your water **consumption.** First, try taking a shower instead of a bath. Showers use a lot less water. You should also turn off the tap while you brush your teeth. Turn it on again to rinse.

I. A good title for this story would be
○ **A.** "How to Brush Your Teeth."
○ **B.** "Saving Water."
○ **C.** "Shower Power."
○ **D.** "The World of Water."

2. In this story the word **consumption** means
○ **A.** running. ○ **B.** bill.
○ **C.** action.   ○ **D.** use.

A. Something is happening to kids in the United States today. They are getting more and more out of shape. Why? Today's kids exercise less.

Many of them don't spend enough time playing sports and games outside. Instead, they sit inside watching TV or using the computer. This can be bad for their health. It's important to exercise. Exercise helps keep your body running smoothly.

Besides, exercise is fun. Playing a sport with other people is much more exciting than watching a TV show alone. So get off that couch and go outside. Join a soccer game or play hide-and-seek. Your body will thank you!

I. According to the story, why are today's kids out of shape?
○ **A.** They don't exercise enough.
○ **B.** They don't watch enough TV.
○ **C.** They play too many sports.
○ **D.** They don't eat well.

2. The purpose of this story is to
○ **A.** inform you that computers are bad.
○ **B.** entertain you with fun and games.
○ **C.** inform you that kids today are in good shape.
○ **D.** persuade you that it's important to exercise.

3. Which of these is an *opinion*?
○ **A.** Many kids today are out of shape.
○ **B.** Not exercising can be bad for your health.
○ **C.** Exercise is fun.
○ **D.** Exercise is good for you.

B. STELLA: I wish I knew what to do for that art project about my neighborhood.

TYRONE: I'm making a collage. I'm going to put in pictures of my neighbors and their homes.

STELLA: That's a great idea. But I don't have any neighbors. In fact, I don't really have a neighborhood. That's why I'm having such a hard time.

TYRONE: How can you not have neighbors or a neighborhood?

STELLA: I live out in the country.

TYRONE: Do you have wild animals where you live?

STELLA: Some. We have raccoons and deer.

TYRONE: Well then, those are your neighbors.

I. Why doesn't Stella think she has neighbors?
  ○ **A.** She lives alone.
  ○ **B.** She lives in the country.
  ○ **C.** She lives with too many animals.
  ○ **D.** She doesn't live near Tyrone.

2. According to the play, which of the following is probably true?
  ○ **A.** Tyrone lives in the city.
  ○ **B.** Tyrone lives in the country.
  ○ **C.** Stella and Tyrone are neighbors.
  ○ **D.** Stella and Tyrone go to different schools.

3. What How are Stella and Tyrone different?
  ○ **A.** One lives in the country and the other doesn't.
  ○ **B.** One has an art project and the other doesn't.
  ○ **C.** One is a raccoon and the other is a deer.
  ○ **D.** One hates animals and the other one loves them.

4. What is Tyrone making?
  ○ **A.** a painting
  ○ **B.** a photograph
  ○ **C.** a painting
  ○ **D.** a collage

C. Do you think a supermarket is only for shopping? Well, think again. In fact, it's a good place to practice your reading skills. Try reading food labels. They're full of information. A label can tell you a lot about what you're eating.

For instance, a label will tell you the ingredients, or what's in the food. The ingredients are listed from greatest to least amounts. Is sugar first or second on the ingredient list? That means the food has a lot of it.

Labels can also tell you how many calories a serving of food has. But be sure to also look at the serving size. A serving of your favorite cookies may have 100 calories. But the serving size may only be one cookie. If you eat four, you're eating 400 calories!

I. If a food has a lot of sugar, where will it be listed on the ingredient list?
  ○ **A.** at the beginning
  ○ **B.** at the end
  ○ **C.** in the middle
  ○ **D.** nowhere

2. Why is it important to know a food's serving size?
  ○ **A.** to know how much it costs
  ○ **B.** to know how much to serve others
  ○ **C.** to know how many calories are in what you eat.
  ○ **D.** to know what the food's main ingredients are.

3. This story will probably go on to talk about
  ○ **A.** more foods that are 100 calories a serving.
  ○ **B.** popular food ingredients.
  ○ **C.** people's favorite cookies.
  ○ **D.** other information available on food labels.

4. What can labels tell you about a food?
  ○ **A.** the size of a serving
  ○ **B.** the number of calories in a serving
  ○ **C.** the ingredients in a food
  ○ **D.** all of the above

D. You're eating pizza at the mall. A friend starts to choke. She is coughing and gasping for air. She can't speak. Would you know what to do?

Carlos Barbosa Jr. did. He performed a lifesaving action called the Heimlich maneuver when he was only 7 years old. He did it after his dad began to choke on some baby carrots.

"I got behind my father and gave his stomach two squeezes," Carlos said. "The carrot popped out of his mouth and flew across the room."

Dr. Henry Heimlich, an Ohio surgeon, developed the Heimlich maneuver 25 years ago. It **dislodges** food that gets stuck in the throat and blocks breathing and speaking. Pressing the stomach forces air out of the lungs. This creates an artificial cough. The rush of air from the cough pushes out the food.

I. What is the Heimlich maneuver?
- ○ **A.** a lifesaving action
- ○ **B.** a way of eating
- ○ **C.** a deathly action
- ○ **D.** a way of choking

2. What happened after Carlos squeezed his dad's stomach?
- ○ **A.** His dad began to choke.
- ○ **B.** His dad began to laugh.
- ○ **C.** Pizza popped out of his dad's mouth.
- ○ **D.** A carrot popped out of his dad's mouth.

3. In this story the word **dislodges** means
- ○ **A.** removes.   ○ **C.** squeezes
- ○ **B.** chokes..   ○ **D.** clogs.

4. From this story you can conclude that
- ○ **A.** people choke all the time.
- ○ **B.** Carlos's dad shouldn't eat carrots.
- ○ **C.** the Heimlich maneuver saves lives.
- ○ **D.** it's dangerous to eat pizza.

E. The movie audience holds its breath. A kid is splashing around in the warm ocean. Suddenly, a shark's fin breaks the surface. It's heading for the unsuspecting swimmer. The background music rises. And then? The kid escapes. And the audience leaves the movie the same way it came in, believing that sharks are evil, people-eating creatures.

The truth is that sharks are neither our enemies nor our friends. Sharks live in every part of the world's oceans, from warm, shallow waters to the darkest depths. They are not evil. But they are fierce **predators.**

In fact, one of the most amazing sights in nature is to watch a shark hunt its prey. First, the shark cruises slowly. When it has its target in sight, it explodes into action. It charges and attacks. Yikes! No wonder sharks have the reputation they do.

But whatever people think of sharks, they must learn to live with these marine creatures.

I. What happens first when a shark hunts?
- ○ **A.** It cruises slowly.
- ○ **B.** It explodes into action.
- ○ **C.** It charges.
- ○ **D.** It attacks.

2. What is the best title for this story?
- ○ **A.** "Scary Scary Sharks"
- ○ **B.** "The Truth About Sharks"
- ○ **C.** "Where Sharks Live"
- ○ **D.** "Good Shark Movies"

3. Which of these is not true about sharks?
- ○ **A.** They live in every part of the ocean.
- ○ **B.** They are good hunters.
- ○ **C.** They are evil.
- ○ **D.** They have fins.

4. In this story, the word **predators** means
- ○ **A.** hunters.   ○ **C.** swimmers.
- ○ **B.** monsters.   ○ **D.** divers.

VOCABULARY

Synonyms

Read the underlined word in each phrase.
Mark the word below it that has the same
(or close to the same) meaning.

Sample:

adore her
- ○ **A.** help
- ○ **B.** harm
- ○ **C.** love
- ○ **D.** hate

1. herd of cattle
   - ○ **A.** sheep
   - ○ **B.** goats
   - ○ **C.** horses
   - ○ **D.** cows

2. gang of people
   - ○ **A.** group
   - ○ **B.** party
   - ○ **C.** crowd
   - ○ **D.** lack

3. with all his might
   - ○ **A.** will
   - ○ **B.** money
   - ○ **C.** strength
   - ○ **D.** desire

4. squeal with joy
   - ○ **A.** cry
   - ○ **B.** squeak
   - ○ **C.** fill
   - ○ **D.** dance

5. boundless energy
   - ○ **A.** unlimited
   - ○ **B.** violent
   - ○ **C.** bright
   - ○ **D.** silly

6. wool and cotton blend
   - ○ **A.** fabric
   - ○ **B.** material
   - ○ **C.** mix
   - ○ **D.** layer

7. resemble him
   - ○ **A.** look like
   - ○ **B.** resent
   - ○ **C.** hate
   - ○ **D.** watch

Antonyms

Read the underlined word in each phrase.
Mark the word below it that means the
opposite or nearly the opposite.

Sample:

swift runner
- ○ **A.** slow
- ○ **B.** fast
- ○ **C.** front
- ○ **D.** small

1. weak arms
   - ○ **A.** thin
   - ○ **B.** fat
   - ○ **C.** strong
   - ○ **D.** soft

2. busy highway
   - ○ **A.** active
   - ○ **B.** quiet
   - ○ **C.** large
   - ○ **D.** major

3. lean and hungry
   - ○ **A.** good
   - ○ **B.** thin
   - ○ **C.** bad
   - ○ **D.** fat

4. flunk the test
   - ○ **A.** fail
   - ○ **B.** take
   - ○ **C.** miss
   - ○ **D.** pass

5. very ordinary
   - ○ **A.** different
   - ○ **B.** nice
   - ○ **C.** orderly
   - ○ **D.** famous

6. adore her
   - ○ **A.** love
   - ○ **B.** hate
   - ○ **C.** like
   - ○ **D.** dislike

7. wintry day
   - ○ **A.** cold
   - ○ **B.** warm
   - ○ **C.** long
   - ○ **D.** tiring

Reading Skills Practice Test 12

READING COMPREHENSION

Read each story. Then fill in the circle that best completes each sentence or answers each question.

Do you know how to stay safe? The No. 1 safety tip is: Never talk to stangers. When you go out, stick to the safest routes. It's also a good idea to tell a parent or another trusted adult where you'll be. If you're home alone, keep all the doors and windows locked.

1. The No. 1 safety tip is
○ **A.** keep doors and windows locked.
○ **B.** stick to the safest routes.
○ **C.** tell you parents where you'll be.
○ **D.** never talk to strangers.

2. From this story, you can conclude that talking to strangers is
○ **A.** dangerous.
○ **B.** interesting.
○ **C.** fun.
○ **D.** safe.

A. The marine toad looks—and acts—like a creature right out of a horror movie. This fat amphibian from South America weighs three pounds and makes a sound like a chugging tractor. When threatened, it oozes poison.

Now, marine toads are terrorizing Florida. They've moved out of the wilds and into the suburbs, where they eat almost anything—small birds, garbage, garden vegetables. They've even developed a taste for pet food!

So how did this monster from South America get to the Sunshine State? In the 1930s, insects were eating the local sugarcane crop. Marine toads were brought to Florida to gobble up the pests. Now the toads have become pests themselves.

1. Why were marine toads brought to Florida?
○ **A.** to be pets
○ **B.** to eat garbage
○ **C.** to be food for pets
○ **D.** to eat insects

2. What is the best title for this story?
○ **A.** "Insects Damage Crops"
○ **B.** "Horror Movies Are a Scream!"
○ **C.** "How to Grow Sugarcane"
○ **D.** "Toad Solution Becomes a Problem"

3. The next paragraph might talk about
○ **A.** other types of toads.
○ **B.** pets in other countries.
○ **C.** how to solve the marine toad problem.
○ **D.** other crops grown in Florida.

B. Who's the biggest athlete in the world? If you're talking size, there's no contest. It's American-born sumo wrestler Salevaa Atisanoe, known in Japan as Konishiki. He tips the scales at 580 pounds.

Sumo wrestling is the national sport of Japan. Thousands of fans attend sumo matches each week. And wrestlers such as Konishiki are treated like movie stars.

What happens at a sumo match? Two sumo wrestlers face each other. There is a lot of pushing and shoving. One wrestler wins when he forces his opponent out of the 15-foot ring, or knocks him to the ground. Each match lasts 20 seconds.

1. What happens first during a sumo match?
○ **A.** They push and shove each other.
○ **B.** They face each other.
○ **C.** One forces the other out of the ring.
○ **D.** One knocks the other to the ground.

2. Which is a *fact*?
○ **A.** Konishiki is the best sumo wrestler.
○ **B.** Sumo wrestling is a fun sport.
○ **C.** Sumo wrestlers should be treated better than movie stars.
○ **D.** Sumo matches last 20 seconds.

3. Salevaa Atisanoe is also known as
○ **A.** Amercia.
○ **B.** Konishiki
○ **C.** Japan.
○ **D.** Sumo.

C. Yellowstone National Park contains some of the most beautiful land in the United States. It has more than 2 million acres of glorious geysers, deep canyons, and vast forests. No wonder it's a top vacation spot.

But many conservationists fear that Yellowstone is becoming a victim of its own success. Increasing numbers of visitors are overcrowding campgrounds and straining park resources. Last year, more than 3 million people packed into the park.

Yellowstone Park may have its problems, but it is also full of success stories—especially for endangered animals like the gray wolf. Thanks to scientists who set up a wolf-breeding program in 1995, gray wolves are roaming free in Yellowstone for the first time in more than 50 years. Wildlife protection laws have also allowed grizzly bears and bison to bounce back from low numbers in recent years.

1. Which of these is an *opinion* about Yellowstone?
○ **A.** It has geysers, canyons, and forests.
○ **B.** It contains some of the most beautiful land in the United States.
○ **C.** Last year, more than 3 million people packed into the park.
○ **D.** Gray wolves are roaming free there.

2. How is Yellowstone different now than it was 10 years ago?
○ **A.** It has fewer visitors and forests.
○ **B.** It's smaller than it was.
○ **C.** It has fewer bison and grizzly bears.
○ **D.** It has more visitors and gray wolves.

3. The main idea of this story is that
○ **A.** Yellowstone Park has both problems and successes.
○ **B.** Yellowstone is a top vacation spot.
○ **C.** Yellowstone Park contains more than 2 million acres.
○ **D.** Gray wolves are endangered.

D. It's important to eat a balanced diet. That means plenty of fresh fruit, vegetables, and grains, but less fat and sugar. A **nutritious** diet helps you feel your best. Then you'll be able to do your best in school and in sports. So say good-bye to fatty cheeseburgers and salty french fries! Say hello to pasta with tomato sauce. What's for dessert? How about some fresh fruit topped with yogurt?

You don't have to change your whole diet overnight. A good way to begin is to try substituting one healthful food for one less healthful food each day. Have your cheeseburger with salad instead of with french fries. The next day, try having oatmeal and fruit for breakfast instead of a sugary cereal. You may be surprised one day to find that you have come to like healthful food as much as the junk food you like now!

I. The main purpose of this story is to
○ **A.** scare.
○ **C.** sell food.
○ **B.** persuade.
○ **D.** amuse.

2. In this story, the word **nutritious** means
○ **A.** high-fat.
○ **C.** sugary.
○ **B.** unhealthful.
○ **D.** healthful.

3. A good way to begin changing your diet is
○ **A.** to eat only candy bars.
○ **B.** to eat only healthful food.
○ **C.** to eat one healthful food instead of a less healthful food each day.
○ **D.** to eat salad at every meal.

4. You can conclude from this story that
○ **A.** high-fat foods are less healthful than lower-fat foods.
○ **B.** everyone likes bananas.
○ **C.** candy bars taste better than apples.
○ **D.** you should never eat foods you like.

E. Jim came over for lunch wearing a blue suit with a short brown tie and a green plaid shirt. I couldn't believe this was going to be my new stepfather. It couldn't be true that my beautiful mother would marry someone who dressed like a clown. I hated him.

Lunch was terrible. Mother kept trying to start a conversation, but neither Jim nor I would say much. Finally, I offered to bring in the dessert just to get away from the clown.

I didn't mean to do it. I guess the plate slipped. But one minute I was handing Jim his blackberry pie, and the next, dark purple berries were oozing all over his shirt and tie.

I was **mortified**. My cheeks turned bright red. Jim looked startled at first, but then he began to laugh. I started laughing too. Maybe this guy was all right, after all. Then I glanced at my mother. She looked happier than I had seen her in a long time.

I. In this story the word **mortified** means
○ **A.** happy.
○ **C.** bored.
○ **B.** angry.
○ **D.** embarrassed.

2. The narrator thinks Jim's clothes look
○ **A.** nice.
○ **B.** expensive.
○ **C.** ridiculous.
○ **D.** old and worn.

3. From the story, you might guess that
○ **A.** Jim didn't seem likeable at first.
○ **B.** the narrator liked Jim from the start.
○ **C.** Jim had no sense of humor.
○ **D.** Jim didn't like blackberry pie.

4. What is the best title for this story?
○ **A.** "I Love Pie"
○ **B.** "My New Stepfather"
○ **C.** "The World's Best Lunch"
○ **D.** "Mothers Shouldn't Marry"

VOCABULARY
Which Word Is Missing?

In each of the following paragraphs, a word is missing. First, read the paragraph. Then find the missing word in the list of words beneath the paragraph. Fill in the circle next to the word that is missing.

Sample:

Jerome's dad belongs to the neighborhood safety association. Last night, it was his turn to _____ the block. He walked up and down all night, keeping everyone safe.

- ○ **A.** sweep
- ○ **B.** leave
- ○ **C.** patrol
- ○ **D.** study

1. When airplanes were first _____ they were small and relatively slow. However, today's jets can go very fast. Some go faster than the speed of sound!

- ○ **A.** improved
- ○ **B.** repaired
- ○ **C.** searched
- ○ **D.** invented

2. One thing that hasn't changed is the seriousness of a pilot's job. A pilot should never be _____. Doing careless or dangerous things risks lives.

- ○ **A.** reckless
- ○ **B.** accurate
- ○ **C.** energetic
- ○ **D.** strict

3. Passengers are certainly more comfortable than they used to be. Old jet planes were very noisy. People used to wear earplugs to keep out the _____.

- ○ **A.** filth
- ○ **B.** music
- ○ **C.** din
- ○ **D.** moisture

4. Airports have changed too. Passengers used to walk onto the runway when getting on and off the plane. Now, upon _____, the plane parks at a gate that leads right inside the airport.

- ○ **A.** transportation
- ○ **B.** landscape
- ○ **C.** publication
- ○ **D.** arrival

5. Many people would say that having chocolate cake for _____ is a great treat. They can't think of a better way to end dinner.

- ○ **A.** lunch
- ○ **B.** delightful
- ○ **C.** dessert
- ○ **D.** menu

6 It's rare that these people will leave even a _____ of chocolate cake on their plates. They want to eat every bite.

- ○ **A.** morsel
- ○ **B.** meager
- ○ **C.** mortal
- ○ **D.** variety

7. For them, a delicious chocolate cake is absolute _____. Nothing could make it better.

- ○ **A.** elegant
- ○ **B.** perfection
- ○ **C.** keen
- ○ **D.** perilous

8. Chocolate is native to the Americas. Its delightfully _____ smell has been making people's mouths water for a long time.

- ○ **A.** fragile
- ○ **B.** fragrant
- ○ **C.** plentiful
- ○ **D.** vivid

9. Today, a chocolate _____ can produce many different products. A chocolate factory might make candy bars, cocoa powder, chocolate-chip cookies, and lots of other delicious treats.

- ○ **A.** gourmet
- ○ **B.** compound
- ○ **C.** manufacturer
- ○ **D.** provision

Reading Skills Practice Test 13

READING COMPREHENSION

Read each story. Then fill in the circle that best completes each sentence or answers each question.

Have you ever seen someone on the beach with a sunburn? A sunburn can be quite painful. If the burn is really bad, the skin might blister and peel. Sunburn is caused by the sun's powerful ultraviolet (UV) rays. Wearing sunscreen can **shield** your skin from those damaging rays.

1. What is the main idea of this story?
- ○ **A.** Ultraviolet rays cause sunburn.
- ○ **B.** Sunburn can cause fever.
- ○ **C.** Sunscreen makes skin peel.
- ○ **D.** The sun is strong at the beach.

2. In this story, the word **shield** means
- ○ **A.** burn.
- ○ **B.** lift.
- ○ **C.** protect.
- ○ **D.** open.

A. For thousands of years, the Inuit people have lived in what is now the northwest part of Canada. For the last 150 years, the Canadian government has ruled the land. Recently, the government has agreed to let the Inuit **govern** part of Canada's Northwest Territory.

Since April 1, 1999, the Canadian map has included the land of Nunavut, which means "our land" in Inuktitut, the Inuit language. The Inuit want control of this land because it is the land of their ancestors. They plan to set up their own government.

1. In this story, the word **govern** means
- ○ **A.** build.
- ○ **B.** rule.
- ○ **C.** map.
- ○ **D.** live.

2. The Inuit language is called
- ○ **A.** Canadian.
- ○ **C.** Nunavut.
- ○ **B.** Inuktitut.
- ○ **D.** Inuit.

3. You can guess from the story that
- ○ **A.** Canada's government once took over Inuit land.
- ○ **B.** Canada's government is unfair.
- ○ **C.** the Inuit cannot speak English.
- ○ **D.** many Canadian people will soon be homeless.

4. Which would come first on a time line?
- ○ **A.** The Inuit make a deal with Canada's government.
- ○ **B.** The Canadian government begins ruling the Inuit's land.
- ○ **C.** The Inuit settle in Canada.
- ○ **D.** Nunavut appears on a map.

B.   Animals depend on plants and other animals for food. The relationship among these animals and plants is called a food chain. The food chain keeps nature in balance. Here's how it works:

1. Producers: Plants and other organisms that provide food for animals make up the first link in a food chain.

2. Herbivores: These are animals that eat only plants. Called "prey," they are hunted by meat eaters.

3. Carnivores: These meat eaters feed on herbivores. They are also called "predators." When they die, their remains fertilize the ground and help plants grow.

1. What is the best title for this story?
- ○ **A.** "Plant-Eating Animals"
- ○ **B.** "Understanding the Food Chain"
- ○ **C.** "Predators"
- ○ **D.** "Plants That Need Animals"

2. Animals that eat meat are called
- ○ **A.** herbivores.
- ○ **C.** prey.
- ○ **B.** producers.
- ○ **D.** carnivores.

3. You can guess from this story that
- ○ **A.** herbivores are hungrier than carnivores.
- ○ **B.** herbivores are small animals.
- ○ **C.** carnivores eat lots of vegetables.
- ○ **D.** each link in the food chain is important.

C.   In Greek mythology, Zeus and Hera were the leaders of the Greek gods. They were husband and wife, and Hera sometimes became angry with Zeus when he spent too much time away from home.

Sometimes, Zeus went to the mountains to play with the forest creatures who lived there. Hera always chased after him because she thought Zeus was wasting time. But every time, a charming creature named Echo chatted with Hera and distracted her until Zeus had escaped.

When Hera figured out that Echo had been tricking her, she was **furious**. "Your talk has made a fool of me!" she screamed. "From now on you will have nothing to say, except what others say to you first!"

From that day on, poor Echo could only repeat the last words of what others said.

1. This story is mostly about
- ○ **A.** Greek gods.
- ○ **C.** Greece.
- ○ **B.** forests.
- ○ **D.** tricks.

2. You can guess from this story that
- ○ **A.** Zeus was tall and handsome.
- ○ **B.** Echo had a loud voice.
- ○ **C.** Hera was very gentle.
- ○ **D.** Echo lived in the forest.

3. In this story, the word **furious** means
- ○ **A.** angry.
- ○ **C.** happy.
- ○ **B.** foolish.
- ○ **D.** tricky.

4. Zeus and Hera were
- ○ **A.** soldiers.
- ○ **C.** forest creatures.
- ○ **B.** married.
- ○ **D.** human.

5. This story is an example of a
- ○ **A.** myth.
- ○ **C.** news article.
- ○ **B.** poem.
- ○ **D.** fairy tale.

D. When you play a sport, do you feel that you must win—or else? The Youth Sports Institute in Michigan surveyed 26,000 boys and girls on this topic, and found that many feel pushed to be the best.

Where does the pressure come from? Some kids put pressure on themselves, but many say that parents and coaches are also to blame. They say these adults care only about the final score—not whether kids tried hard or had a good time.

I. What is the main idea of this article?
○ A. Fewer kids should play baseball.
○ B. Youth sports are always fun.
○ C. Many kids feel a lot of pressure to win at sports.
○ D. Parents should be banned from going to kids' games

2. Which of these statements is a *fact*?
○ A. Sports pressure is the worst part of kids' sports.
○ B. The Youth Sports Institute surveyed 26,000 kids.
○ C. Winning is important.
○ D. Coaches should not be allowed to pressure players.

3. The author wrote this article to
○ A. tell why baseball is good exercise.
○ B. tell kids to quit playing sports.
○ C. tell about the history of youth sports.
○ D. tell about a problem in youth sports.

4. The article probably goes on to talk about
○ A. solving the problem of sports pressure.
○ B. baseball training camps for kids.
○ C. ways for teams to win more games.
○ D. youth football programs.

E. In 1844, young Elizabeth Blackwell dreamed of becoming a doctor. There was just one problem: No medical school in the U.S. would accept a woman as a student. Blackwell convinced several doctors to teach her privately. Then, in 1847, she was accepted by a small college in New York. She graduated at the top of her class.

Blackwell traveled to Paris, France, where she studied at a hospital. Even after losing her sight in one eye, Blackwell did not give up her work as a doctor. In the 1850s, she returned to the U.S. and **established** a hospital for women and children. Today, we remember Elizabeth Blackwell as the trailblazer who opened the field of medicine for women in America.

I. In this story, the word **established** means
○ A. set up.   ○ C. named.
○ B. cured.   ○ D. lost.

2. What is the best title for this story?
○ A. "Elizabeth Blackwell: Opening College Doors"
○ B. "Elizabeth Blackwell: First Woman Doctor"
○ C. "The Autobiography of Elizabeth Blackwell"
○ D. "Famous Doctors in History"

3. Which of these is an *opinion*?
○ A. Blackwell lost sight in one eye.
○ B. Blackwell became a doctor.
○ C. Blackwell lived in the 1800s.
○ D. Blackwell was very brave.

4. You can guess from this story that Elizabeth Blackwell
○ A. got good grades in college.
○ B. had French parents.
○ C. eventually became totally blind.
○ D. died in 1860.

VOCABULARY
Which Word Is Missing?

In each of the following paragraphs, a word is missing. First, read the paragraph. Then find the missing word in the list of words beneath the paragraph. Fill in the circle next to the word that is missing.

Sample:

The car suddenly stopped in the middle of the road. It had run out of ____. The driver had forgotten to fill up the gas tank.

- ○ **A.** miles
- ○ **B.** fuel
- ○ **C.** water
- ○ **D.** popcorn

The driver was late for his soccer game. That was too bad, because he was the best ____ on his team. His teammates counted on him to stop the other team from scoring.

- ○ **A.** coach
- ○ **B.** goalie
- ○ **C.** gardener
- ○ **D.** catcher

1. Some really large animals live on the plains of Africa. You might think the biggest ones would be the mightiest hunters, but that's not the case at all. Some of the world's biggest animals eat nothing but leaves, grasses, and shrubs. Instead of hunting other animals, these huge creatures ____ on plant life to survive.

- ○ **A.** dwell
- ○ **B.** sit
- ○ **C.** grow
- ○ **D.** graze

2. The largest plant eater of all is the African elephant. In fact, the African elephant is the largest land ____ in the entire world! An adult elephant can weigh as much as 12,000 pounds. And a baby elephant is not exactly tiny: It can weigh up to 250 pounds at birth!

- ○ **A.** shark
- ○ **B.** soil
- ○ **C.** mammal
- ○ **D.** farmer

3. Another very large African plant eater is the white rhinoceros. It is second in size only to the elephant. The adult white rhino can weigh up to 5,000 pounds, or two-and-a-half ____.

- ○ **A.** dollars
- ○ **B.** tons
- ○ **C.** ounces
- ○ **D.** feet

4. The black rhino is a ____ of the white rhino. Although the two are kin, the black rhino doesn't get nearly as large. At 3,000 pounds, though, the adult black rhino is still pretty big. Both rhinos are very good at using their horns to break off tree branches for dinner.

- ○ **A.** relative
- ○ **B.** neighbor
- ○ **C.** friend
- ○ **D.** killer

5. A somewhat smaller African plant eater is the hippopotamus. At 700 pounds, the adult hippo seems almost ____ compared with an elephant or a rhino—but you'd still feel pretty small standing next to one! A hippo has teeth about 20 inches long. They are excellent tools for munching coarse plants.

- ○ **A.** giant
- ○ **B.** desperate
- ○ **C.** dainty
- ○ **D.** loyal

6. The hippo's teeth also come in handy for fighting off crocodiles. That's important, because hippos spend lots of time in rivers, where crocs live. Hippos have sensitive skin that can easily get too dry. They hang out in the river to keep their skin ____.

- ○ **A.** nasty
- ○ **B.** moist
- ○ **C.** brown
- ○ **D.** clean

Reading Skills Practice Test 14

READING COMPREHENSION

Read each story. Then fill in the circle that best completes each sentence or answers each question.

SAMPLE

During a 1992 storm, a ship lost thousands of plastic turtles, frogs, and ducks in the Pacific Ocean. Since then, the toys have drifted thousands of miles. Some have shown up in the ocean off of Alaska. The toys' trip helps scientists study how wind affects drifting objects.

I. A good title for this story would be
○ **A.** "Drifting Toys."
○ **B.** "The Great State of Alaska."
○ **C.** "The Big Storm."
○ **D.** "Turtles in the Sea."

2. Scientists study the toys to find out about
○ **A.** how turtles swim.
○ **B.** how wind affects drifting objects.
○ **C.** how far it is from Russia to Alaska.
○ **D.** how ducks find food.

A. Ten-year-old Caitlin Gionfriddo makes money in a funny way. She chews Gummi Worms, tastes peanut butter, and chomps on chocolate.

Caitlin has more than a big appetite. The fifth-grader from Cincinnati, Ohio, helps companies dream up new flavors, names, and colors for their products.

"When kids design things, it's what kids want, not what adults want," says Caitlin.

To understand what kids want, companies need to think like kids. So they hire them. For instance, when Curad was looking for a new kid bandage design, they went straight to the experts. They asked 25 kids what they wanted to put on their cuts and bruises. The kids came up with ideas for fun bandages. Then a cartoonist sketched the ideas. The winner? Tattoo bandages.

I. Why did Curad hire 25 kids?
○ **A.** They wanted them to taste Gummi Bears.
○ **B.** They wanted them to taste chocolate.
○ **C.** They wanted them to help design a new bandage.
○ **D.** They wanted them to help design a new toy.

2. The main purpose of this story is to
○ **A.** inform you about why companies hire kids.
○ **B.** persuade you to eat more peanut butter.
○ **C.** amuse you with details about Caitlin's life.
○ **D.** explain how bandages are designed.

3. You can conclude from this story that
○ **A.** Companies don't care what kids think.
○ **B.** Caitlin really hates what she does.
○ **C.** Companies are out of touch with today's kids.
○ **D.** Products designed for kids are important to companies.

B. Tiny ocean **creatures** with horse-shaped heads may seem like characters from a fairy tale. But sea horses are real. And, they're in real danger.

The World Conservation Union, a group that protects nature, has said that sea horses are in danger of becoming extinct. That means that soon there may be no more sea horses left in the world's oceans.

Sea horses are curly-tailed fish. They are usually no more than a few inches long. Though small, they're in big demand. Some people collect the odd-looking fish. Others eat them. They're also used in Chinese cures for skin diseases and other illnesses.

Fishermen from Florida to the Philippines support their families by selling sea horses. But overfishing causes the loss of at least 20 million sea horses each year. If something isn't done, the only horses on the planet will be the ones left on dry land.

1. What is the best title for this story?
   ○ **A.** "All Kinds of Horses"
   ○ **B.** "Disappearing Sea Horses"
   ○ **C.** "What To Do with Sea Horses"
   ○ **D.** "Fishing Around the World"

2. In this story, the word **creatures** means
   ○ **A.** animals.
   ○ **B.** plants.
   ○ **C.** boats.
   ○ **D.** waves.

3. Why are sea horses disappearing?
   ○ **A.** They are being eaten by other fish.
   ○ **B.** They are being overfished.
   ○ **C.** They are too small to survive in the ocean.
   ○ **D.** They are suffering from a disease.

C. Students in the city of Houston, Texas, are climbing the walls. They're not bored. They're working out!

These days, sports like rock climbing are hot in gym class. Hundreds of physical education programs across the country now offer students all sorts of sports. In-line skating, aerobics, mountain biking, and hiking top the list.

According to the experts, kids ages 4 to 12 should exercise for 60 minutes or more each day. But kids won't exercise if they don't enjoy it. So physical education teachers have found new ways to make exercise fun. For some kids, this means harder and more exciting sports, like rock climbing. For others, it means making activities less competitive. One teacher replaced her school's 1-mile run with a 12-minute run. That way, everyone finishes at the same time. Even slow runners can enjoy themselves.

1. According to the story, how long should kids exercise each day?
   ○ **A.** 12 minutes
   ○ **B.** 4 minutes
   ○ **C.** 60 minutes
   ○ **D.** 30 minutes

2. What is the best title for this story?
   ○ **A.** "Gym Is Great"
   ○ **B.** "A New Kind of Gym Class"
   ○ **C.** "Dodge Ball"
   ○ **D.** "Rainy Day Activities"

3. From this story, you can guess that
   ○ **A.** it's important to exercise.
   ○ **B.** it's important to be good at sports.
   ○ **C.** gym classes are boring.
   ○ **D.** most schools don't have gym classes.

D. Stop. Extreme danger. Access strictly **prohibited**. These warnings greet scientist Tim Dixon as he goes to work each day. Dixon works on El Popocatépetl (Poh-poh-kah-tep-eh-tuhl). El Popo, as it's known, is one of the most dangerous volcanoes in the world.

Dixon is putting special equipment on the Mexican volcano. He hopes the equipment will help scientists predict future eruptions. He has already discovered how surprising El Popo can be. "We were up there when, without warning, there was a large blast," he says. "We felt the shock waves hit us. Then, we saw red-hot pieces of rock falling down." But Dixon was fortunate. The eruption was small. It only lasted a few minutes. He wasn't hurt.

El Popo's last big eruption was 1,200 years ago. It killed many people. Dixon and other scientists want to make sure it doesn't happen again. They hope that before the next big eruption, there will be time to warn people.

1. What happened after Dixon felt shock waves on El Popo?
- ○ **A.** Red-hot pieces of rock fell down.
- ○ **B.** Many people were killed.
- ○ **C.** There was a large blast.
- ○ **D.** Dixon's equipment was ruined.

2. In this story, the word **prohibited** means
- ○ **A.** special
- ○ **B.** expensive
- ○ **C.** not watched
- ○ **D.** not allowed

3. Why is Dixon putting special equipment on El Popo?
- ○ **A.** He wants to keep it from erupting.
- ○ **B.** He wants to collect some red-hot rocks.
- ○ **C.** He wants to make it erupt more often.
- ○ **D.** He wants to predict future eruptions.

E. How does getting lowered into the ground by your ankles sound? That's what one worker had to do to reach three ancient mummies in Argentina. It was worth it, though. The mummies were in "near-perfect" condition. Now scientists want to use them to learn about the past.

The mummies are the remains of three kids who died 500 years ago. They were buried under dirt and rock on top of a volcano. There are two girls and a boy. It's hard to tell the exact age of a mummy, but scientists know that the kids were between 8 and 15 years old when they died. No one is certain how they died.

Scientists hope the mummies will help them learn more about the Inca civilization. The Inca were an ancient South American people. They had a huge empire that lasted over 100 years. The mummies may reveal new information about the Inca.

1. Which of these is an *opinion*?
- ○ **A.** There are two girls and a boy.
- ○ **B.** It was worth it, though.
- ○ **C.** No one is certain how they died.
- ○ **D.** The Inca were an ancient South American people.

2. Which is the best title for this story?
- ○ **A.** "The Ancient Inca"
- ○ **B.** "Three New Mummies"
- ○ **C.** "How Mummies Are Made"
- ○ **D.** "Volcanoes in Argentina"

3. According to the story, why are the mummies important?
- ○ **A.** They are in "near-perfect" condition.
- ○ **B.** They are very young.
- ○ **C.** Scientists don't know how they died.
- ○ **D.** Scientists can use them to learn more about the Inca.

VOCABULARY

Synonyms

Read the underlined word in each phrase. Mark the word below it that has the same (or close to the same) meaning.

Sample:

tilt the picture
- ○ **A.** straighten
- ○ **B.** turn
- ○ **C.** hang
- ○ **D.** frame

---

1. building site
- ○ **A.** place
- ○ **B.** time
- ○ **C.** event
- ○ **D.** window

2. stout person
- ○ **A.** skinny
- ○ **B.** heavy
- ○ **C.** loud
- ○ **D.** small

3. big victory
- ○ **A.** loss
- ○ **B.** win
- ○ **C.** smile
- ○ **D.** frown

4. uncover the truth
- ○ **A.** hide
- ○ **B.** find out
- ○ **C.** cover up
- ○ **D.** change

5. solemn face
- ○ **A.** smiling
- ○ **B.** happy
- ○ **C.** unhappy
- ○ **D.** serious

6. shield your face
- ○ **A.** protect
- ○ **B.** hide
- ○ **C.** wipe
- ○ **D.** hurt

7. startled expression
- ○ **A.** puzzled
- ○ **B.** surprised
- ○ **C.** unhappy
- ○ **D.** bothered

Antonyms

Read the underlined word in each phrase. Mark the word below it that means the opposite or nearly the opposite.

Sample:

unkind words
- ○ **A.** mean
- ○ **B.** nice
- ○ **C.** angry
- ○ **D.** funny

---

1. bright room
- ○ **A.** dim
- ○ **B.** loud
- ○ **C.** large
- ○ **D.** airy

2. thorough cleaning
- ○ **A.** detailed
- ○ **B.** careful
- ○ **C.** careless
- ○ **D.** yearly

3. tremendous force
- ○ **A.** great
- ○ **B.** very little
- ○ **C.** scary
- ○ **D.** unbelievable

4. unfriendly people
- ○ **A.** mean
- ○ **B.** kind
- ○ **C.** strange
- ○ **D.** unfamiliar

5. terrible time
- ○ **A.** happy
- ○ **B.** great
- ○ **C.** boring
- ○ **D.** surprising

6. ancient treasure
- ○ **A.** sunken
- ○ **B.** gold
- ○ **C.** new
- ○ **D.** expensive

7. graceful dancer
- ○ **A.** clumsy
- ○ **B.** ballet
- ○ **C.** light
- ○ **D.** young

Reading Skills Practice Test 15

READING COMPREHENSION

Read each story. Then fill in the circle that best completes each sentence or answers each question.

SAMPLE

The Canadian province of Manitoba has a rather snaky reputation. That's because thousands and thousands of red-sided garter snakes gather there every winter. Most snakes can't live as far north as Manitoba. The winters are just too cold. But red-sided garter snakes have a way of keeping warm. Every year they slither into an area in central Manitoba. There they pack themselves into underground dens. One den might hold more than 20,000 snakes!

1. What is the best title for this story?
○ **A.** "All About Manitoba"
○ **B.** "All About Snakes"
○ **C.** "Winter in the Far North"
○ **D.** "Red-Sided Garter Snakes"

2. Why can't most snakes live in the far north?
○ **A.** The winters are too cold.
○ **B.** There aren't enough underground dens.
○ **C.** The red-sided garters attack other snakes.
○ **D.** They are not allowed into Manitoba.

A. On May 13, 1607, colonists from England landed their boats on an island that is now part of Virginia. They built a settlement there. They called it Fort James—and later Jamestown—in honor of the king of England.

Life in Jamestown was difficult. The settlers suffered from disease and hunger. The winters were very cold. **Disputes** with neighboring settlements made life in Jamestown dangerous. Many people died. But the survivors did not give up. When their fort burned down, they rebuilt it and made it larger. The colonists stayed in Jamestown for almost 100 years.

1. What happened first?
○ **A.** The colonists built Fort James.
○ **B.** The colonists died from disease and hunger.
○ **C.** The colonists rebuilt Fort James after it burned down.
○ **D.** The colonists landed on an island.

2. In this story, the word **disputes** means
○ **A.** ceremonies.   ○ **C.** illnesses.
○ **B.** fights.   ○ **D.** discussions.

3. What is the main idea of this story?
○ **A.** Life in Jamestown was difficult.
○ **B.** The colonists rebuilt the fort that burned down.
○ **C.** Winters in Jamestown were very cold.
○ **D.** The settlers died from disease and hunger.

B. Everyone knows that salads are delicious and good for you. But making a salad can seem tricky to some people. How do you make a good salad? Just follow these tips:

- Always dry your lettuce or spinach after washing it. Salad dressing won't stick to wet leaves.
- Just lettuce and tomatoes make an okay salad. But why not perk it up with some other vegetables? Try carrots, cucumbers, or mushrooms.
- Try adding a can of beans to your salad. They're tasty, and they make the salad even more nutritious.
- Go easy on the salad dressing. It should complement the taste of the vegetables, not **conceal** it.

1. What is one reason it's good to add beans to salad?
- ○ **A.** Salad dressing sticks to them.
- ○ **B.** Salad isn't tasty without them.
- ○ **C.** They make salad more nutritious.
- ○ **D.** They hide the taste of salad dressing.

2. In this story, the word **conceal** means
- ○ **A.** hide.
- ○ **B.** reveal.
- ○ **C.** control.
- ○ **D.** close.

3. What is the best title for this story?
- ○ **A.** "Salad-Making Tips"
- ○ **B.** "How to Wash Lettuce"
- ○ **C.** "How to Make Salad Dressing"
- ○ **D.** "Why Salad Is Good for You"

C. Imagine the most famous person you know of. Michael Jordan. Britney Spears. Prince William. Now think of this: Not one of them is as famous as Helen Keller was in her day.

When she was a baby, Helen Keller became blind and deaf because of an illness. Helen's family didn't think she would ever learn to communicate well. But they didn't count on Helen's teacher, Annie Sullivan. Annie taught Helen to speak and to communicate through sign language. She also taught Helen to read and write Braille, an alphabet system used by blind people. Annie made the world open up for Helen.

Word of Helen's learning spread quickly. She became famous, and people all over the country wanted to meet her. Helen went on to graduate from college, travel the world, and write 13 books. When she died, at the age of 87, she had become one of America's great heroes.

1. Why did Helen Keller become so famous?
- ○ **A.** She was a famous author.
- ○ **B.** She was Annie Sullivan's student.
- ○ **C.** She did not let disabilities stop her from achieving her goals.
- ○ **D.** She met famous people and traveled the world.

2. What would Helen's life have been like without Annie Sullivan?
- ○ **A.** She may not ever have been able to communicate.
- ○ **B.** She would have been famous anyway.
- ○ **C.** Her parents would have taught her to read and write.
- ○ **D.** She would have grown up like any other kid.

3. Which of these is the best comparison for how Annie Sullivan changed Helen's life?
- ○ **A.** a car crashing
- ○ **B.** a bubble bursting
- ○ **C.** a rock falling
- ○ **D.** a flower opening

D. Mariel didn't see the new girl coming toward her on the sidewalk until it was too late. She bumped right into the girl, sending books flying everywhere.

"Oh excuse me!" she cried. "I'm so sorry. I didn't see you!"

The new girl smiled. "That's okay. I didn't see you either. I'm Shamala. What's your name?"

"I'm Mariel. Where did your family move here from?"

"We came from Chicago. But before that we lived in Houston. And before that we lived in Santa Ana. And I was born in India, so I guess we lived there too, but I was too young to remember."

"Wow, you've lived in a lot of places. I've lived here in the same house all my life. You're really lucky."

Shamala laughed. "That's funny. I was just thinking that you're the lucky one!"

I. Why did Mariel bump into Shamala?
- ○ **A.** She didn't like Shamala.
- ○ **B.** Shamala was new.
- ○ **C.** She didn't see Shamala coming.
- ○ **D.** Shamala had lived in a lot of places.

2. How are Mariel and Shamala alike?
- ○ **A.** They are both new in the neighborhood.
- ○ **B.** They have both lived in a lot of places.
- ○ **C.** They are both unfriendly.
- ○ **D.** They both envy the other one's life.

3. What is most likely to happen next in this story?
- ○ **A.** Mariel and Shamala never see each other again.
- ○ **B.** Mariel and Shamala become friends.
- ○ **C.** Mariel's family moves.
- ○ **D.** Mariel and Shamala become enemies.

E. The year is 1912. The day is April 10. The *Titanic* sets sail from England. The enormous ship is three football fields long. Eleven stories high, it is the largest moving object ever built. The ship has elegant restaurants, a swimming pool, and indoor gardens. Some of the world's richest people stroll through its fine rooms. No one seeing it at this moment would guess that tragedy lies ahead.

It is the ship's first voyage. This floating palace is bound for New York City. The crew intends to set a record getting there. The *Titanic* is the most powerful ship on the sea, brags its builder. There is nothing to fear. Let other ships' crews worry about iceberg warnings. Other ships aren't the *Titanic*. The *Titanic* is **unsinkable**.

Sadly, pride goes before the fall. Around midnight on April 14, 1912, a massive iceberg rips open the mighty ship's steel hull. Tons of water gush in. For the *Titanic*, the end has come.

I. In this story the word **unsinkable** means
- ○ **A.** luxurious.   ○ **B.** large.
- ○ **C.** heavy.   ○ **D.** buoyant.

2. The *Titanic* was
- ○ **A.** made of stone, just like a palace.
- ○ **B.** filled with luxuries such as swimming pools and gardens.
- ○ **C.** a large restaurant that had been fitted to float.
- ○ **D.** just like every other ship of the time.

3. Which adjective best describes the Titanic's builder?
- ○ **A.** excited
- ○ **B.** modest
- ○ **C.** proud
- ○ **D.** deceitful

4. What is the purpose of this story?
- ○ **A.** to entertain you with details of the *Titanic* tragedy
- ○ **B.** to scare you into avoiding big ships
- ○ **C.** to help you picture what the *Titanic* was like
- ○ **D.** to persuade you that the *Titanic's* builder was cruel.

VOCABULARY
Which Word Is Missing?

In each of the following sentences, a word is missing. First, read the paragraph. Then find the missing word in the list of words beneath the paragraph. Fill in the circle next to the word that is missing.

Sample:

It was getting late, so they _____ their pace.

○ **A.** ambled   ○ **C.** quickened
○ **B.** measured   ○ **D.** slowed

1. He was _____ around new people and didn't talk much.

○ **A.** bold   ○ **C.** angry
○ **B.** timid   ○ **D.** antsy

2. If this _____ weather continues, we will need to turn up the heat.

○ **A.** balmy   ○ **C.** frigid
○ **B.** pleasant   ○ **D.** sweltering

3. It is good to be _____ of others, no matter how different they are.

○ **A.** tolerant   ○ **C.** suspicious
○ **B.** critical   ○ **D.** wary

4. The mystery of who took his lunch continued to _____ him.

○ **A.** surprise   ○ **C.** baffle
○ **B.** delight   ○ **D.** excite

5. Their _____ was about whose turn it was to clean up after dinner.

○ **A.** dispute   ○ **C.** assignment
○ **B.** occasion ○ **D.** encounter

6. "Follow that car!" the woman shouted _____.

○ **A.** quietly   ○ **C.** contentedly
○ **B.** frantically ○ **D.** blissfully

7. She was _____ in her decision and never regretted it.

○ **A.** wavering   ○ **C.** discouraged
○ **B.** steadfast ○ **D.** disappointed

8. The beautiful painting was _____ by a large black mark on it.

○ **A.** created   ○ **C.** helped
○ **B.** attacked ○ **D.** marred

9. He was always _____, shaking hands and thanking everyone.

○ **A.** tragic   ○ **C.** tasteful
○ **B.** cordial   ○ **D.** remote

10. Despite being dropped three times, the television made it upstairs _____.

○ **A.** shattered ○ **C.** roundly
○ **B.** happily   ○ **D.** intact

11. My friend's _____ the way I draw realistic-looking animals.

○ **A.** admire ○ **C.** ignore
○ **B.** pity   ○ **D.** scorn

12. She was _____ about moving to a new town where she knew nobody.

○ **A.** thrilled ○ **C.** anxious
○ **B.** jealous   ○ **D.** mean

13. He loves to write so much that we _____ he will be a writer when he grows up.

○ **A.** explain ○ **C.** regret
○ **B.** predict ○ **D.** ignore

Answer Key

TEST 1
Sample: 1.D 2.C

Passage A
1.D 2.A 3.D

Passage B
1.C 2.A 3.C

Passage C
1.C 2.D 3.A 4.B

Passage D
1.A 2.B 3.D

Passage E
1.A 2.D 3.D 4.B

Vocabulary
Synonyms
Sample: A
1.C 2.B 3.B 4.C
5.D 6.B 7.A
Antonyms
Sample: C
1.C 2.D 3.D 4.C
5.A 6.B 7.A

TEST 2
Sample: 1.D 2.C

Passage A
1.C 2.D 3.B

Passage B
1.C 2.D 3.B

Passage C
1.B 2.A 3.C 4.C

Passage D
1.B 2.C 3.B

Passage E
1.B 2.C 3.D

Vocabulary
Synonyms
Sample: C
1.B 2.B 3.C 4.D
5.B 6.D 7.B

Antonyms
Sample: C
1.D 2.D 3.A 4.C
5.C 6.C 7.A

TEST 3
Sample: 1.D 2.A

Passage A
1.B 2.D 3.C

Passage B
1.B 2.B 3.D

Passage C
1.C 2.A 3.B 4.D

Passage D
1.A 2.B 3.D 4.C

Passage E
1.B 2.C 3.A

Vocabulary
Synonyms
Sample: B
1.C 2.A 3.B 4.B
5.D 6.D 7.B
Antonyms
Sample: A
1.C 2.D 3.A 4.D
5.B 6.C 7.D

TEST 4
Sample: 1.D 2.C

Passage A
1.C 2.B

Passage B
1.A 2.D 3.A

Passage C
1.C 2.B 3.B

Passage D
1.A 2.D 3.D

Passage E
1.C 2.C 3.B

Vocabulary
Synonyms
Sample: D
1.D 2.A 3.B 4.C
5.D 6.B 7.A
Antonyms
Sample: A
1.D 2.C 3.A 4.B
5.D 6.B 7.A

TEST 5
Sample: 1.B 2.A

Passage A
1.D 2.A 3.C

Passage B
1.A 2.D 3.C

Passage C
1.B 2.B 3.D

Passage D
1.C 2.B 3.B

Passage E
1.B 2.B 3.C

Vocabulary
Synonyms
Sample: A
1.C 2.B 3.D 4.B
5.D 6.D 7.C
Antonyms
Sample: B
1.B 2.B 3.A 4.B
5.A 6.D 7.C

TEST 6
Sample: 1.B 2.D

Passage A
1.A 2.C 3.A

Passage B
1.C 2.A 3.C

Passage C
1.D 2.A 3.C

Passage D
1.C 2.B 3.A

Passage E
1.C 2.D 3.B

Vocabulary
Synonyms
Sample: A
1.D 2.B 3.C 4.B
5.A 6.A 7.D
Antonyms
Sample: B
1.B 2.A 3.B 4.D
5.B 6.D 7.C

TEST 7
Sample: 1.B 2.C

Passage A
1.C 2.C 3.B

Passage B
1.D 2.C

Passage C
1.D 2.B

Passage D
1.C 2.D 3.A

Passage E
1.A 2.B 3.A 4.D

Passage F
1.B 2.A 3.B

Vocabulary
Synonyms
Sample: A
1.B 2.C 3.B 4.D
5.D 6.B 7.A
Multiple Meanings
Sample: C
1.B 2.D 3.B 4.A

TEST 8
Sample: 1.B 2.A

Passage A
1.C 2.B 3.A 4.C

Passage B
1.C 2.A 3.D

Passage C
1.D 2.C 3.B 4.C 5.D

Passage D
1.D 2.A 3.C 4.B

Passage E
1.B 2.D 3.B

Vocabulary
Synonyms
Sample: A
1.C 2.B 3.D 4.C
5.A 6.A 7.A
Antonyms
Sample:B
1.B 2.A 3.D 4.A
5.C 6.C 7.B

TEST 9
Sample: 1.B 2.B

Passage A
1.B 2.C 3.A

Passage B
1.B 2.D 3.C

Passage C
1.C 2.B 3.D 4.B

Passage D
1.D 2.A 3.C

Passage E
1.C 2.B 3.D

Vocabulary
Synonyms
Sample: B
1.A 2.D 3.C 4.A
5.B 6.A 7.D
Antonyms
Sample: C
1.A 2.D 3.A 4.A
5.A 6.A 7.D

TEST 10
Sample: 1.C 2.C

Passage A
1.B 2.C

Passage B
1.A 2.C 3.B

Passage C
1.C 2.A 3.C

Passage D
1.B 2.A 3.D

Passage E
1.C 2.A 3.B 4.B

Vocabulary
Synonyms
Sample: A
1.D 2.B 3.D 4.B
5.D 6.B 7.C
Antonyms
Sample: A
1.B 2.B 3.D 4.A
5.A 6.A 7.B

TEST 11
Sample: 1.B 2.D

Passage A
1.A 2.D 3.C

Passage B
1.B 2.A 3.A 4.D

Passage C
1.A 2.C 3.D 4.D

Passage D
1.A 2.D 3.A 4.C

Passage E
1.A 2.B 3.C 4.A

Vocabulary
Synonyms
Sample: C
1.D 2.A 3.C 4.B
5.A 6.C 7.A
Antonyms
Sample: A
1.C 2.B 3.D 4.D
5.A 6.B 7.B

TEST 12
Sample: 1.D 2.A

Passage A
1.D 2.D 3.C

Passage B
1.B 2.D 3.B

Passage C
1.B 2.D 3.A

Passage D
1.B 2.D 3.C 4.A

Passage E
1.D 2.C 3.A 4.B

Vocabulary
Sample: C
1.D 2.A 3.C 4.D
5.C 6.A 7.B
8.B 9.C

TEST 13
Sample: 1.A 2.C

Passage A
1.B 2.B 3.A 4.C

Passage B
1.B 2.D 3.D

Passage C
1.A 2.D 3.A 4.B 5.A

Passage D
1.C 2.B 3.D 4.A

Passage E
1.A 2.B 3.D 4.A

Vocabulary
Which Word Is Missing?
Sample:B; B
1.D 2.C 3.B
4.A 5.C 6.B

TEST 14
Sample: 1.A 2.B

Passage A
1.C 2.A 3.D

Passage B
1.B 2.A 3.B

Passage C
1.C 2.B 3.A

Passage D
1.A 2.D 3.D

Passage E
1.B 2.B 3.D

Vocabulary
Synonyms
Sample: B
1.A 2.B 3.B 4.B
5.D 6.A 7.B
Antonyms
Sample: B
1.A 2.C 3.B 4.B
5.B 6.C 7.A

TEST 15
Sample: 1.D 2.A

Passage A
1.D 2.B 3.A

Passage B
1.C 2.A 3.A

Passage C
1.C 2.A 3.D

Passage D
1.C 2.D 3.B

Passage E
1.D 2.B 3.C 4.C

Vocabulary
Which Word Is Missing?
Sample: C
1.B 2.C 3.A 4.C 5.A
6.B 7.B 8.D 9.B
10.D 11.A 12.C 13.B